BEST
GOLF COURSES

FLORIDA'S BEST GOLF COURSES

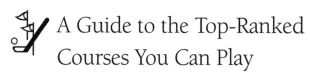 A Guide to the Top-Ranked
Courses You Can Play

Ronnie Ramos
Assistant Sports Editor
The Miami Herald

THE MIAMI HERALD

ANDREWS AND McMEEL
A Universal Press Syndicate Company
Kansas City

For my wife Connie,

who said I could play.

And play. No one else

is so lucky.

*Florida's Best Golf Courses: A Guide to the
Top-Ranked Courses You Can Play*
© 1995 by Ronnie Ramos. All rights reserved.
Printed in the United States of America. No part of
this book may be used or reproduced in any manner
whatsoever without the written permission of Andrews
and McMeel except in the case of reprints in the context
of reviews. For information write to Andrews and McMeel,
a Universal Press Syndicate Company, 4900 Main Street,
Kansas City, Missouri 64112.

Additional copies of this book may be ordered by
calling (800) 642-6480

Library of Congress Cataloging-in-Publication Data

Ramos, Ronnie.
    Florida's best golf courses : a guide to the top-ranked
  courses you can play / Ronnie Ramos.
        p.   cm.
    ISBN 0-8362-0568-5   (pbk.)
    1. Golf courses—Florida—Directories.   I. Title.
GV982.F5R36 1995   95-37350
796.352'06'8759—dc20   CIP

CONTENTS

THANKS

It would be impossible to thank by name all the people who helped make this book, but there are some I must mention.

Stephanie and Kevin Hayes. In exchange for playing many of Florida's greatest courses with me, Kevin had to endure my talking about them. And Stephanie had to endure both of us. Everyone should have such good friends.

And to my family, for their support, especially my sister Gloria for her copy editing help.

There were dozens of people at golf courses and resorts throughout the state who patiently answered all my questions, provided photographs and politely answered more questions. Among them, Kirsten Reed at Sandestin, Ramona Hurley and Alexandra Shontz at Innisbrook, Bill Reid at TPC–Sawgrass and Penina Freedman at Amelia Island Plantation.

A special thanks to the excellent panelists, who graciously agreed to help nominate courses.

And thanks to Betty Grudzinski of the *Miami Herald*, who believed in this project from the start, edited every word and came up with countless excellent suggestions to improve the book.

INTRODUCTION

THE MOST DIFFICULT task is trying to explain what makes a great golf course. I had this conversation with dozens of people during the past year as I researched this book. The answers ranged from the stringent dependence on physical criteria—conditioning, surroundings, amenities, etc.—to the undefinable.

The pornography test was mentioned several times: I can't define it, but I know it when I see it.

It gets a little trickier when it comes to determining which course is greater than another. One panelist mentioned that history has to play a significant role; being able to play where the pros play—and where they made historic shots—elevates a course. He had a point, because six of the top eight courses host a PGA, LPGA or Senior PGA tour event.

I think it is a combination of physical characteristics (that is what the panelists used to nominate courses) and the unmeasurable characteristics (that is part of what I used to determine the Top 100 order).

Tom Fazio, who knows how to design great courses (four of his courses are ranked in the top 11) said one of his goals is that you remember the course after you're done playing. "One of the things we work hard on is memorability," he said. "Even if you played well or poorly, wouldn't it be nice if you remember those holes? The challenge is not to go overboard in creating uniqueness."

One of the best debates on what makes a great golf course took place, interestingly enough, on the front nine of the TPC–Stadium Course. At the time, none of us knew it would turn out to be the top-ranked course.

I was playing with panelists Joe Oglesby and Kevin Hayes, who has played many of the top 50 courses in this book with me.

We had played Long Point at Amelia Island the day before and we had all agreed it was the most beautiful course in Florida. There is no better setting for a golf course. It was perfectly maintained and there were many memorable holes, including two along the Atlantic Ocean.

As we played the front nine at TPC, I asked them how they would compare this course to Long Point. It is difficult, because they are so different. The Stadium Course is massive in every regard, from the clubhouse to the land around the holes. Long Point is charming and secluded, its clubhouse a tiny thing with a glorified snack bar.

Joe voted for Long Point, saying it had more real character. His point was that the Stadium Course was created character, with its severe mounding and bulkheaded greens. You had to be precise on every shot, too precise.

Kevin tended to agree with Joe, but he wondered about the Players Championship that was held on the Stadium Course each year and the historical significance of the course.

The conversation drifted to other subjects as we made the turn.

It came back quickly when we turned the bend on No. 16 and looked out to the right and saw the island green of No. 17 in the middle of the lake. Standing on the tee on No. 17, we talked about Tiger Woods' amazing birdie on this hole to essentially win the U.S. Amateur.

The pin was near the spot where it was that day. Joe was the only one to put his first shot on the green. But not even that convinced him.

A group of 80 panelists nominated their top five courses from their region of the state. Of all the regions, there was no closer battle for No. 1 than in the Northeast, between the TPC–Stadium Course and Long Point. Almost every panelist in that region had these two courses ranked 1 or 2. TPC–Stadium Course barely won. But I suspect the debate will continue.

I still haven't told Joe which course came out No. 1 in this book. I do know which one would be No. 1 in his book.

In trying to explain what makes one course great and another very good, it may help to understand the word *duende*. It is a Spanish word that is hard to define because there is no real translation. It is used to define people, but I submit that it can be used to describe golf courses as well.

The *Real Academia de la Lengua*, sort of the *Webster's* of Spain, defines *duende* as "mysterious and ineffable charm." A bullfighter has *duende* when he displays not bravery, but unmistakable class.

But it is more than class. James Michener, in his book *Iberia*, credited Goethe, who writing about something else, with this definition:

"That mysterious power which all sense but no one can explain."

Sometimes it is better to explain it in terms of who has and doesn't have *duende*. It is possible to have it for a period of time and then lose it. Jack Nicklaus had it in the 1960s and '70s, but not today. Arnold Palmer had it when he walked up No. 18 at Oakmont Country Club in 1994, at the end of his final round in the U.S. Open.

John Daly has never had it, not even when he won his first—and only—major.

Ben Crenshaw most definitely had it on the back nine of Augusta in 1995. Nick Faldo, Nick Price, Tom Watson and Fred Couples don't even know it exists.

Seve Ballesteros has it, but Jose Maria Olazabal doesn't.

Among golf courses I have played, *duende* exists at No. 3 at Medinah. It drips from the moss-covered oaks and surrounds the greens. There are better courses and prettier ones, but I suspect there is none with more *duende*. Augusta has it, not at Amen Corner, where it is too far from the gallery to draw much emotion, but on No. 10, a spiraling downhill par 4 in a secluded corner of the course that descends through majestic trees. It may be the most charismatic hole I have ever seen.

In Florida, Long Point comes the closest to having it. All over the place.

It exists in specific spots throughout the state, places where time stands still and you get this strange feeling you can't describe. Such as behind the first and 10th tees on the Copperhead Course at Innisbrook. Or the No. 9 tee box (the back one) at Ravines. Or the 17th hole at the TPC–Stadium Course. And not because it is so famous, but because you can play the exact shot the pros play and experience it the way they do.

Golden Ocala has the poor man's version, if such a thing is possible; Copperhead has the resort version and Bay Hill has the course-surrounded-by-houses kind. At Bay Hill, you get the unmistakable feeling *duende* is just around the next bend (or maybe it's the feeling Arnold Palmer, who lives here part of the year, may be in one of the foursomes ahead of you).

And Pine Barrens may have it by next year. Which means I should do an updated version of the book so I can go check.

ABOUT THE AUTHOR

RONNIE RAMOS is an assistant sports editor at the *Miami Herald*. He has been playing golf for 10 years, never as well as he would like. Ramos, a 14-handicap, writes golf travel stories and is editor of *South Florida Golf* magazine, which covers golf in Southeast Florida.

He learned to play at Granada Golf Course, a nine-hole municipal in Coral Gables. The course, which opened in 1924, is the oldest nine-hole course in Florida. It has one design element critical for beginning golfers: no water. Since then, he has played more than 100 golf courses in Florida, as well as dozens more in six other states.

Ronnie Ramos and his wife Connie have two children, Natalie and Christopher. They live in South Miami.

ABOUT THIS BOOK

If it doesn't work out, there will never be any doubt
That the pleasure was worth all the pain.

— Jimmy Buffett

A T SOME POINT, not long after I became addicted to this game, I began fascinated with the incredible number of golf courses in Florida. It seemed there were all these great golf courses in the middle of nowhere.

The numbers are astounding: more than 1,100 courses in Florida at the end of 1994, more than 600 of them are public access. No other state has as many golf courses as Florida (California is second).

Several major golf publications, such as *Golf Digest* and *Golf* magazine, rate the best courses in the country and the best courses in a half-dozen other categories. But most of those lists are loaded with private courses many of us will never see the first tee of.

What are the top courses in Florida you can play?

Now you know.

The pleasure was getting out and playing golf courses all over the state. The pain was ranking them.

I have played more than 100 courses in Florida, including 25 of the top 30 courses in this book. There are dozens more I didn't play, but spend some time looking at them. I visited all 100 courses ranked in this book and I have played 73 of them.

Many times I played courses with strangers who had great stories to tell. Such as Terry Inslee, a golf nut who ranks courses for *Golf Digest*. We played Burnt Pine in the Panhandle with Matt Lindley, the head pro there.

Then there were the father and son from Britain I was matched up with at Pelican's Nest in Southwest Florida. They forgot their suntan lotion and were baked pretty well by the time our afternoon round was done.

Playing new courses can be a challenge. I'll never forget the time I went with a friend to play Grand Palms, just west of Ft. Lauderdale.

We were paired with two older members of the course and my friend kept asking them, on every tee, "Where's the hole?"

By the 14th hole, my friend asked again, "Where's the hole?" "Right underneath the flag," one of the senior slammers replied, without smiling.

Overall, it was an unforgettable experience. The trip to Jacksonville with two panelists, Kevin Hayes and Joe Oglesby, is a good example. We played six golf courses in four days and drove over 300 miles in between. The sun never shone, it was cold, rainy and windy—and we had a blast.

Another instance: I convinced another panelist, Hans Deryk, to get up at 5 A.M. and drive to Emerald Dunes (No. 10) in West Palm Beach. On the 18th tee, with another 18 holes still to play elsewhere, he said it was worth it. I couldn't agree more.

The Book

This book is broken down into three sections. The first section outlines the five regions we divided the state into: Southeast, Southwest, Central, Northeast and Northwest. Part two is the Top 100 courses ranked in order. In the third part, we break the rankings down by region, provide a detailed map of the area and include 65 other notable courses throughout the state.

The Rankings

Each of the 80 panelists nominated five courses in their region. I also talked with more than 100 golfers around the state about their favorite courses. A few panelists who had traveled extensively throughout the state were asked to nominate their top five courses in the state.

The panelists rated each course in their region in eight categories: character, challenge, condition, design, memorable holes, setting, service and amenities. The panelist must have played the course within the past year. If a panelist worked for a public access course, his or her nomination of that course was not used.

This process yielded the top 20 to 30 courses within each region.

I then ranked the courses from 1 to 100 using those ratings. I repeat, the rankings are mine, not the panelists.'

Ranking golf courses is subjective. Your ranking of the Top 100 would probably be different. What I tried to do here was give you a feeling for the different courses in Florida and tell you something about them before you play them.

Here are some things I can say about the Top 100 courses in this book:

They are all in excellent condition. They all have memorable holes or a wonderful setting that will stick in your mind long after your round. They all have several very good golf holes that will challenge you and demand the best from your game.

And most importantly, they are all courses I want to play tomorrow.

The Scorecard

Each course—there are 165 listed in this book—has a scorecard which includes the course's address, phone number, par and yardage. Under access, we listed how you can get on. Some courses restrict when the public can play and others require that you stay at their hotel or resort.

The green fees are a price range. As Floridians know, there are two golf seasons in Florida, winter and summer. In most places, the winter season runs from November to April and the summer season lasts from May to October. The difference? About half. As a rule of thumb, courses cut their prices in half during the summer.

The best example is Saddlebrook Resort outside Tampa. The course is open to the public year-round, but it can be tough to get a tee time in the winter, when resort guests take most of them—and green fees are as high as $135. In the summer, "we basically give the place away," one pro told me. During the summer, Saddlebrook is under $30 and accepts several of the charity golf cards that allow you to play area courses for discounted rates.

Many of the excellent resorts also offer great deals in the summer, with packages that include hotel room and a round of golf for under $100. The days are longer and getting 36 holes a day in is no problem. It is also hotter, much hotter. You decide.

It is wise to call before you visit any course to get exact green fees and verify access. While I was compiling this book, three public courses decided to go private.

Excuses, Errors, Omissions

This book took more than a year to research and compile. I talked to more than 200 people about their favorite golf courses in the state. I collected more than 50 local and regional publications to keep up with opening and closing courses.

I realize I may have missed one. OK, maybe two. We tried to make this book as inclusive as possible. No one paid to be included. If we left out a course you think should in the Top 100, please let me know. Or if you want to send me your top 10 in Florida or your region, feel free. You can write to Ronnie Ramos, Miami Herald, 1 Herald Plaza, Miami, Florida 33132.

THE PANELISTS

THE MEN AND WOMEN who agreed to help with this book have only two things in common: they love to play golf and have played many different courses in their region. They all volunteered. There are golf writers and golf pros, old and young players. There are some who do the ratings for golf courses and others who coordinate tournaments all over the region.

There is a member from both the LPGA and PGA tours. And there are golfers like you and me, some who struggle to break 100, others who strive to break 90. They have handicaps from 0 to 25.

The panelists did not know how courses were ranked before this book was published. The individual nominations of each panelist also will not be disclosed.

Panelist	Profession	City	Hdcp.
Barry Adeeb	Owner, Adeeb's Sea Turtle Inn	Atlantic Beach	8
Emilio Alvarez	Manufacturer's representative	Miami	18
Mark Arrington	District sales manager, USAir	Fort Myers	2
Chuck Bombard	Head golf professional, TPC–Sawgrass	Ponte Vedra Beach	0
Guy Boros	PGA Tour player	Ft. Lauderdale	0
Charles Callaghan	President, Florida First Coast of Golf	Jacksonville	10
Pat Cattanach	Head golf professional, Lely Flamingo	Naples	0
Keith Carwell	Banker	Davie	16
Dick Clark	Director, Golf Daytona Beach	Daytona Beach	13
Mike Clayton	Head golf professional, University Park	Sarasota	0
W. Earl Daniel	Golf course rating coordinator, FSGA	Gulf Breeze	4
Jim Deaton	Head golf professional, Bay Hill	Orlando	0
Charles DeLucca	Golf professional	Miami	0
Hans Deryk	Photographer, Associated Press	Ft. Lauderdale	8
John B. Downs	Physician	Naples	1
Mick Elliott	Golf writer, *Tampa Tribune*	Tampa	18
Will Frantz	Golf professional, Country Club of Ocala	Ocala	0

Panelist	Profession	City	Hdcp.
Larry Gantzer	Golf professional, Naples Beach Resort	Naples	0
Don Green	Owner, Golf USA stores	Jacksonville	1
C.M. Guerrero	Photographer, *Miami Herald*	Miami	10
Mary Hafeman	Head golf professional, Ponce de Leon	St. Augustine	0
Jim Hall	Food broker	Lakeland	10
Bob Harig	Golf writer, *St. Petersburg Times*	St. Petersburg	16
Nancy Harrison	Director, Emerald Coast Golf Association	Pensacola	
Kevin Hayes	Real estate appraiser	Lakeland	15
Calton Henderson	Publisher, *Gulf Coast Tee Times*	Pensacola	12
Wayne Holland	Owner, title insurance company	Tampa	15
Don Hollenback	Regional publisher, *Golfer's Guide*	Jacksonville	8
Mike Jamison	Freelance golf writer	Lake Mary	9
Bill Janney	Regional publisher, *Golfer's Guide*	Naples	18
Tracy Kerdyk	LPGA Tour player	Coral Gables	0
Joseph Kesner	Executive director, Palm Beach County Golf Association	West Palm Beach	8
Bill Kilpatrick	Golf writer, *Ft. Myers News-Press*	Ft. Myers	10
Kathy Lawrence	Manager, Halifax Plantation	Ormond Beach	0
Matt Lindley	Head gold professional, Burnt Pine	Destin	0
Richard LoGello	Medical sales representative	Orlando	8
Marty Martinez	Head professional, Deer Creek	Deerfield Beach	0
Bret Mason	Golf writer, *Ft. Pierce Tribune*	Ft. Pierce	16
Steve Melnyk	Developer	Jacksonville	2
Rafael Miguel	Anesthesiologist	Tampa	21
Stephen Monahan	Project manager, Ravines	Middleburg	12
Jim Montgomery	Owner, public relations firm	North Miami	11
Nat Moore	Golf events coordinator; former Miami Dolphins receiver	Miami	7
Carlos Morales	Marketing director, Golf Club of Miami	Miami	8
John Norton	Head golf pro, Golf Club of Miami	Miami	0
Joe Oglesby	Assistant managing editor, *Miami Herald*	North Miami	15
Doug Oselett	Editor, Southwest Florida Golf	Ft. Myers	2
Jose Paneda	Spanish radio broadcaster, Miami Heat	Miami	14
Pat Paolini	President, St. Augustine Chamber	St. Augustine	16

Panelist	Profession	City	Hdcp.
Paige Phillips	Golf professional, LPGA International	Daytona Beach	0
Ted Raymond	Golf writer, *Northwest Florida Daily News*	Ft. Walton Beach	7
Bill Reid	General manager, TPC–Sawgrass	Ponte Vedre Beach	0
Craig Rhodes	Private investigator	Ft. Lauderdale	8
Steve Riviere	Banker	Apopka	2
Ernie Rodriguez	Pharmaceutical sales	Miami	15
Bill Rose	*Tropic Magazine* editor, *Miami Herald*	Miami	7
Roger Schafer	Retired	Mulberry	19
Allan Schwartz	Retired	Miami	21
Fred Seely	President, Florida Golf Foundation	Jacksonville	7
Dave Sheinin	Golf writer, *Miami Herald*	Hollywood	25
Campbell Smith	Publisher, *North Florida Golf News*	Jacksonville	5
Chris Smith	Golf writer, *Florida Times-Union*	Jacksonville	12
Herb Smith	Senior PGA Tour player	Miami	0
Tom Spousta	Golf writer, *Sarasota Tribune*	Sarasota	12
Roscoe Staples	General manager, Deercreek	Jacksonville	1
Tom Stine	Publisher, *Golfweek*	Kissimmee	8
Barry Turnball	Owner, golf marketing company	Jacksonville	7
Bill Vilona	Golf writer, *Pensacola News-Journal*	Pensacola	15
David Varlotta	Anesthesiologist	Tampa	13
Billy Varn	Forest products — investments	Jacksonville	1
Robert von Hagge	Golf course architect	Houston, Texas	0
Kay Vawter	Retired	Jacksonville	12
Jim Warters	Freelance golf writer	West Palm Beach	18
Tom Weaver	Head golf professional, Marriott Bay Point	Panama City Beach	0
George White	On-air golf analyst, The Golf Channel	Orlando	14
Jim Williams	Cart man, Country Club of Ocala	Ocala	0
Ken Willis	Golf writer, *Daytona Beach News-Journal*	Daytona Beach	15
David Wilson	Deputy sports editor, *Miami Herald*	Pembroke Pines	13
Kenny Winn	Head golf professional, Falcon's Fire	Kissimmee	0
Jim Witherspoon	Tournament director, Florida State Golf Association	Sarasota	4

FLORIDA'S REGIONS

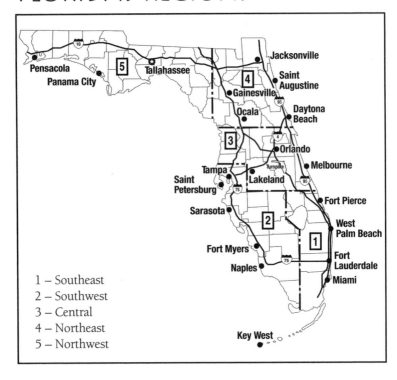

Jacksonville

Pensacola
Panama City

5 Tallahassee

4 Saint
Augustine

Gainesville

Ocala

Daytona
Beach

3 Orlando

Tampa

Saint
Petersburg

Lakeland

Melbourne

Sarasota

Fort Pierce

2 West
Palm Beach

Fort Myers

1 Fort
Lauderdale

Naples

Miami

Key West

1 – Southeast
2 – Southwest
3 – Central
4 – Northeast
5 – Northwest

FLORIDA'S REGIONS

F ROM THE BUSTLING CLAMOR of Miami to the peaceful white sands of
the Panhandle beaches, Florida enjoys a hard-to-match diversity
of landscape and culture. The golf courses are just as varied, from the
flat, mangrove-lined fairways in Southeast and Southwest Florida, to
the steep hills and moss-covered oak trees that define courses in
Northeast Florida.

In this book, Florida is divided into five regions to help you lo-
cate the golf courses in your area.

SOUTHEAST REGION

From the ritz of rich Palm Beach to the glamour of South Beach,
Southeast Florida is home to Jack Nicklaus, Sly Stallone, Greg Norman, Madonna and Raymond Floyd.

It also is home to two PGA Tour and two Senior Tour events (and
you can play all four courses where the tournaments will be held in
1996), the PGA of America national headquarters and the 1,000th
golf course to open in Florida.

Situated along the Atlantic Ocean, the region reaches from Key
West to Vero Beach and includes the most populated part of the state,
including Miami, Ft. Lauderdale, Hollywood and West Palm Beach.

In Southeast Florida, good golf holes and good courses are indis-
putably tied to how well they incorporate water into their designs:

■ The best municipal golf course in Florida (Key Biscayne) is on an
island.

■ The best golf hole in the region (No. 18 at Doral's Blue Course)
owes its fame to the lake lining its left side.

■ And the most picturesque par 3 in the region (at Ft. Lauderdale's
Bonaventure Resort) requires you to hit over a waterfall.

Southeast Florida lacks the spectacular resort courses of Central
and Northeast Florida, but it is the easiest place to play where the
pros play.

Doral's Blue Course, home of the Doral-Ryder Open, is open to
the public. Doral is the largest golf resort in the state, with four regu-

lation courses at the same site. The Honda Classic is moving to Heron Bay in Coral Springs, a daily fee course scheduled to open in early 1996.

The Links at Key Biscayne, home of the Senior PGA Tour's Royal Caribbean Classic, is a county-run course. The Champions Course at PGA National, home of the PGA Championship, is open to resort guests.

Emerald Dunes, course number 1,000 to open in Florida, is an upscale daily fee course designed by the most popular golf course architect in the world today, Tom Fazio.

There are also a handful of public courses that have hosted PGA Tour events throughout the years. Miami Springs Golf Course is where Byron Nelson began his incredible streak of 11 consecutive Tour wins in 1945. The Biltmore Golf Club (No. 50) was the site of the biggest purse—$10,000—on the PGA Tour in the 1930s. Jack Nicklaus played his first pro event in 1961 at what is now the Golf Club of Miami's West Course (No. 29).

SOUTHWEST REGION

Southwest Florida has the most remarkable collection of courses you can just walk on and play. There are two Tom Fazio courses, a pair of Robert Von Hagge classics, one of the few Robert Trent Jones Sr. designs in the area and a dozen Ron Garl creations.

One of the Tom Fazio courses, Pelican's Nest just north of Naples in Bonita Springs, was a pioneer in upscale public golf. It was one of the first courses to offer country club amenities—free range balls, free yardage books, coolers filled with ice on every cart—at daily fee prices.

The region is among the largest in area, from the Marco Island/Naples in the south area up along the Gulf of Mexico past Bradenton and Sarasota and up to the St. Petersburg/Tampa Bay area.

It easy to see why Pelican's Nest drew rave reviews from the panel; it combines the best natural setting of any course in the region with fabulous maintenance.

With less fanfare and a completely different look, Eastwood in Fort Myers is Southwest Florida's version of Southeast Florida's Links at Key Biscayne. Both are municipal courses designed by Von Hagge and they are the two highest-rated municipal courses in the state.

But if ever a region was stamped with the personality of one architect, Southwest Florida is Ron Garl country.

You can start in Naples and drive north on I-75 and visit several of his creations. He did some of the renovations at the Naples Beach Resort; Olde Hickory in Ft. Myers, University Park in Sarasota, The River Club in Bradenton, Buffalo Creek in Palmetto and Bloomingdale outside Tampa. The list goes on and on. Garl has designed 15 courses in Southwest Florida alone, including two of the premier private courses, Fiddlesticks in Ft. Myers and TPC at Prestancia.

If you want a resort, there is Innisbrook, the best pure golf resort in Florida. With three great courses—including the No. 2 course in Florida—nestled in a forest and the friendliest staff in the state, Innisbrook is golf heaven. It is a ski resort for golfers. Pure, great golf unspoiled and unhurried.

You can follow in the pros' footsteps at Innisbrook's Copperhead, where the PGA and LPGA Tours come for the J.C. Penney Classic, or walk on to the TPC at Tampa Bay, a Senior PGA Tour stop.

CENTRAL REGION

Jack Nicklaus, Tom Fazio, Pete Dye and Rees Jones—four of the best golf course architects today—have all built great courses in Central Florida. Blessed with year-round great weather, elevation changes (by Florida standards) and lots of room, Central Florida has the best collection of public-access golf courses in Florida and is second only to Chicago for the best in the country.

Six of the top 20 courses in Florida's Top 50 are in Central Florida, more than any other region. Central Florida also placed 14 courses in the Top 50, also more than any other region.

The region stretches from the Atlantic Ocean to the Gulf of Mexico along Florida's midsection. It includes Melbourne on the east coast, Brooksville near the west coast, Ocala to the north and Orlando, Lakeland, Kissimmee and Haines City in between.

You know golf is big business here when Walt Disney World—best known for its Magic Kingdom and Epcot Center—has five courses and plans to build more. Joe Lee built the first three courses, Pete Dye built Eagle Pines and Tom Fazio built the crown jewel, Osprey Ridge.

There are famous resorts with great golf courses, such as Grand

Cypress, Bay Hill and Grenelefe. And there are great golf courses in the middle of nowhere, such as World Woods and Golden Ocala.

Gone are the old "Florida-style" golf courses—flat with lots of water and sand. Central Florida has seen some innovative designs that are setting the standard all over the country.

Nicklaus raised eyebrows when he unveiled his North/South Course at Grand Cypress. He transformed a flat, lifeless piece of land into a hilly, incredibly contoured course with greens and tees high in the sky and raised fairways. He later came back and created a Scottish course—with no trees and only a dab of water—that is among the best in the country.

Rees Jones is also two-for-two here. At LPGA International, he designed a course specifically designed for professional women, built from the middle back. He also designed Falcon's Fire, which has developed into the prototype upscale daily fee facility.

The golf boom continues unabated here. New golf courses open almost monthly. Among them, Falcon's Fire opened in 1993, LPGA International and Gary Player's Baytree National in Melbourne opened in late 1994, and Diamondback, a Joe Lee design in Haines City, opened in early 1995.

NORTHEAST REGION

Anchored by two world-class resorts and blessed with some of the best daily fee facilities in the state, Northeast Florida is giving Central Florida a good run as the top golf destination in the state.

Certainly it is the best organized. A not-for-profit organization called Florida's First Coast of Golf (800-877-PUTT) was established in 1992 and has evolved into a strong promoter of the area. The group has put together golf packages with 26 area hotels, condos and resorts and with 22 golf courses. A full-color, 45-page brochure—free for the asking—shows you every hotel, every course and lists dozens of golf packages.

The region stretches from the Florida–Georgia border down the Atlantic Ocean to just south of Daytona Beach. Amelia Island and the Jacksonville area make up most of the golf in this region.

The Northeast region has much to tout. There are courses along the ocean, courses along the Intracoastal Waterway and courses winding through forests and wetlands. There is Florida's top-ranked course—the TPC–Stadium Course. There is Florida's best resort, Amelia Island Plantation. And there is Florida's best mountain course (we did say Florida!), Ravines.

Ravines, southwest of Jacksonville in tiny Middleburg, may be the most fun course in Florida to play. Those accustomed to mountain courses may not understand the hoopla, but to those born and bred on Florida's flat water-laden tracts, this course is a thrill. You must hit shots across deep ravines, off sides of hills to greens on other hills, across rivers and straight uphill.

Less than an hour away is Marriott's Sawgrass Resort, the king of Florida golf with three courses in the Top 50: the top-ranked TPC–Stadium Course, the TPC–Valley Course and Sawgrass Country Club. The Stadium Course, controversial when it first opened, has emerged as a Pete Dye classic and the one course everyone still talks about.

Less than 15 minutes away is the Ocean Course at Ponte Vedra Inn, home of what is believed to be the world's first island green, the par 3 ninth.

Farther north up the coast is Amelia Island Plantation, a private little island world detached from the rest of the world. If you can go to only one resort, go here. Tom Fazio's Long Point course is the most beautiful course in the state, and the other 27 holes of Amelia Links—all Pete Dye creations—are also superb. You are right on the ocean, on wonderful beaches with unspoiled sand dunes as a backdrop that blocks out civilization.

NORTHWEST REGION

The region's eastern border is Tallahassee, the state's capital, and goes west to the Florida-Alabama border. In the 60 miles between Panama City and Pensacola lies one of the finest stretches of beaches in the United States. Quiet, unspoiled and rarely crowded, the Panhandle, dubbed the Emerald Coast, draws most of its visitors to the beaches.

The golf courses are the same: quiet, unspoiled and rarely crowded. The Panhandle doesn't have the high-profile golf resorts prevalent throughout the rest of the state. But the not-as-famous resorts have the added advantage of being on or next to the beach—a major attraction for family vacations and something Grand Cypress, Doral and Innisbrook cannot offer.

You can stay on the beach midway between Pensacola and Panama City—in Destin, Navarre or in tiny but spectacular Seaside—and almost every good course in the region is less than an hour's drive away.

Almost every course in Northwest Florida qualifies as a hidden gem to most golfers.

Drive Highway 98 from Panama City west to Pensacola and you will stumble across many gems.

Hurry and go play Sandestin's Burnt Pine Golf Club, the latest and best creation in Florida by Rees Jones. Jones, who also recently finished LPGA International in Daytona Beach and also designed the acclaimed Falcon's Fire down the road from Walt Disney World, succeeded in his mission: "We set out to build the best course in this part of the country."

Sandestin, an oceanfront, three-course complex just west of Destin, is the largest resort in the region. Burnt Pine will eventually become a private course, but for now you can play it if you stay at the resort.

Ron Garl, he of the long, snaking bunkers, created one of his best Florida courses in Hidden Creek. The course, in Navarre just west of Pensacola beach, hosts U.S. Open qualifying rounds.

Before he became the hottest architect in the world, Tom Fazio carved a beautiful layout through the woods of Niceville that became the original 18 holes of Bluewater Bay Resort. No. 3 on what is now the Lake Course is probably the best par 4 in the region.

Northwest Florida is also home to Jerry Pate's original jewel, Tiger Point East. Pate designed it and was the pro there before selling it.

THE TOP 100
FLORIDA'S COURSES RANKED

1
TPC–STADIUM COURSE
MARRIOTT AT SAWGRASS RESORT

It is the site of the biggest PGA Tour event in Florida. It has the most famous golf hole in Florida, if not the U.S. It is the most famous course in Florida. It is also one of the most controversial.

Since the day it opened in 1980, the greatness of the innovative Stadium Course has been debated with fervor. Is it too tricked up, with little character? Or is it a great test of golf, one that lays your game—and its flaws—bare for you to assess?

Pete Dye conceived and built TPC as a major tournament course, one that would serve as the home club for the members of the PGA Tour. It was also to be the permanent home of the Players Championships, that Tour stop two weeks before The Masters that desperately wants to become golf's fifth major.

At the time it opened, the course was full of innovations, most notably the elevated viewing areas around many holes and the grass bleachers around the 17th and 18th greens. The elevated mounds down the right side of the 18th hole alone can accommodate 40,000 fans.

Then there is the No. 17, the most-photographed hole in golf and excepting Amen Corner at Augusta and the shoreline at Pebble Beach, the most famous golf hole in the United States.

But unlike those other beauties, the Stadium Course's No. 17 has a special appeal almost no other famous hole can match. It is one of the few holes in the world where you can easily play it *exactly* like the pros. The hole, with its island green, is only 132 yards from the back tees, and it's a shot even the high handicappers feel they can hit.

Stand on the 18th at Doral's Blue Course, the wind in your face, and try to cut the corner of the water like the pros do on Sunday. Or on 18 at Pebble Beach, and tell yourself to aim to the lone tree on the right side and draw it back toward the ocean. Most of us can't do that and the rest of the hole sets up differently.

But at the TPC–Stadium Course, stand there on No. 17 tee, the wind slightly in your face, staring at the island green, bulkheaded on

all sides and with no room for
error, and you get a rare chance to
experience exactly what the pros
do. It's only 132 yards, you tell
yourself, and the green is not that
small.

It's just you and your pitching
wedge. Or your 9-iron. Or maybe
the 8-iron. Or a 7-iron, because the
wind is blowing. Naw, the 8-iron, I
can't afford to go over. And therein
lies the lure of No. 17. It is not just
the water or the island green. It's
that, for one shot at least, No. 17 is
a hole you can experience just like
the pros do.

On the other 16 holes, however,
you could use their drives, their
short game and their putting. The
course is target golf, the critics will
say. It's a shotmaker's course, those
who love it will say. You better be
accurate, everyone will agree.

No. 17

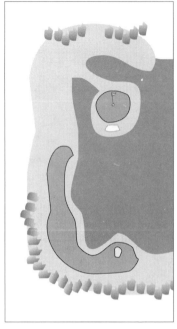

Par 3, 132 yards.

If this course has a weakness, it's the first three holes, which do
not take your breath away. Get your pars here because they will be
hard to come by after No. 3.

The rough is penal and the landing areas are small. But there is
usually more than one option of which way to attack on many holes,
especially the par 5s. Other than Pine Barrens (see No. 3), this is a
great collection of par 5s. On No. 9, a creek cuts across the fairway
halfway out, forcing you to decide where to hit on your second shot.
A huge bunker runs along the left side and water runs all along the
right side.

No. 11 requires thought before playing. The fairway tails right,
with a huge waste bunker all along the left side. There is a second
fairway on the left side that begins about 150 yards in front of the
green. Depending on where the pin is, you may want to hit your second shot over the massive waste bunker to the green on the left. Or

No. 11 on the TPC Stadium Course has it all: water, sand and a very tough green to hold.

you can continue up the green on the right, but your approach will have to carry a small lake and a big bunker.

No. 16 is a par 5 that is real tough to reach in two shots and you probably have to hit three different shots. Your tee shot must fade to be placed between a bunker on the right and the trees on the left, far enough right to give you a good second shot.

Your second shot will probably be a draw to get you on the left side for the best approach to a green that sticks out in the lake like a peninsula. With water right, and a hump in the middle of the green, your approach must stop quickly on the right tier.

The Stadium Course has the best three finishing holes in Florida, with a reverent nod to Bay Hill, which comes in a strong second. Besides the just-mentioned No. 16 and the famous No. 17, the finishing hole is a cross between No. 18 at Pebble Beach and No. 18 at Doral, the best closing hole in Florida. Like both of those, this No. 18 has water on the left and the hole turns left around the water. It is 440 yards from the back tees (420 blue, 351 white) and the slightly elevated green is tough to hold.

With this kind of finish, the most famous par 3 in Florida, some of the fastest and toughest greens to putt and one of the best maintained courses in the state, the Stadium Course is a great golf course.

Is it the best? Play it yourself and decide. One thing is certain. When you are done you will have a definite opinion, one way or another. You cannot leave here indifferent about the debate.

S C O R E C A R D

Region: Northeast

Address: 1000 TPC Boulevard, Ponte Vedra Beach (20 miles southeast of Jacksonville.)

Phone: (904) 285-7777

Access: Marriott resort guests only.

Yardage/Slope:

Tournament: 6,857 yards / 135

Back: 6,394 yards / 130

Middle: 5,791 yards / 126

Forward: 5,034 yards / 123

Par: 36/36, 72

Green fees: $100 and up.

What the Panelists said:

"Tour showcase—it shows; worth the money." —Stephen Monahan (12).

"Has become more playable for amateur and professional golfers with changes in course over last several years. The area's only showcase course you can brag about playing." —Barry Turnball (7)

"The prototype of 'modern' course architecture, for better or worse. The TPC's difficulty is its appearance; it's scary to look at with the sand waste areas, mounds and water. Very difficult course for the average player." —Fred Seely (7)

"Severe challenge from the back tees. You feel you are part of PGA Tour history when you play here." —Billy Varn (1)

"Best known, most controversial course in area, but it has matured into a top-rate course. No. 17 is best-known, but it is solid from beginning to end." —Chris Smith (12)

"Every hole has character. You have to put the ball in the proper position off the tee to score." —Don Green (1)

"Most challenging course in America." —Don Hollenback (8)

2
COPPERHEAD COURSE
INNISBROOK HILTON RESORT

There is no place in all of Florida better than the hilltop between the first and 10th tee on the Copperhead Course. Some courses have signature holes. This place has a signature feeling. Innisbrook is golf, pure and simple, no tricks, no waterfalls, no man-made mogul-track.

And all you need to see to understand this is that hill between No. 1 and No. 10.

On one side, the long dogleg par 5 opening hole stretches down the hill, a daunting bunker in the middle of the fairway 210 yards from the green. On the other side, the tenth hole, a long par four with a narrow fairway, snakes through tall pines and oaks.

The first time I played Copperhead was the time I fell in love with golf for good. A friend and I had finished playing the Island Course late in the day. We mentioned to a pro we had never seen Copperhead. He said it was late, but if we wanted to play the back nine, go ahead.

Summer was ending, there was not a cloud in the sky and the sun was dropping. There was no one else on the course. There was no other sound. Playing that back nine, hitting tee shots down huge hills, hearing the sound of your shots echo through the trees, was an almost mystical experience. We raced the setting sun to the 18th green.

The next time I played Copperhead, the place was packed. I had an early tee time and was with another friend. I had him stand on that hill. He froze. "This is incredible," he half-whispered, as if he would disturb the setting.

Innisbrook grabs you that way. Just north of Tampa, the resort is in an isolated wooded setting. It's like a ski resort for golfers. The suites are clustered in different buildings, tucked away in the woods. There are three courses, all in the Top 100—Copperhead, Island (No. 27) and Sandpiper (No. 87), which has three nines. Each has its own clubhouse.

Along with Grand Cypress in Orlando and Marriott's Sawgrass Resort in Jacksonville, Innisbrook is one of the top golf resorts in the state. It has the most charm and is the best value of the three. The summer packages at Innisbrook, which start at under $100, are the best overall deal in Florida. But be forewarned: You can only play the courses if you stay at the resort.

Home of the annual J.C. Penney Classic, a combined PGA and LPGA event, the Copperhead Course is an E. Lawrence Packard design that rolls up and down hills. Its beauty and immaculate conditions captivate you and its winding fairways and unique holes challenge you.

Copperhead has unusual elevations for a Florida course, and there is little water on the course. But the tree-lined fairways and myriad of bunkers make this a very tough course.

Holes 14–16 are the best examples of Copperhead's charm:

No. 14, par 5 (572 yards, 548, 527, 507): A downhill double dogleg coils right at the end and drops dramatically to a green guarded in the front and right by a pond and on the left by the largest bunker on the course. The pond begins 120 yards out and the fairway slopes toward the water, so your second shot must be carefully placed.

No. 15, par 3 (212 yards, 182, 162, 147): You tee off from an elevated tee to a green that appears to be in a pit. The hole plays about 10 yards shorter because of the elevation drop. The green is huge and slopes from right to left. A beautiful hole.

No. 16, par 4 (458 yards, 423, 402, 304): The hardest hole on the course, it doglegs right around a lake. There is not much of a corner to cut off and your second shot is a long one to a wide green with no trouble in front, but two nasty bunkers on each side.

No. 14

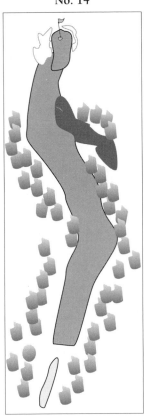

Par 5, 572 Yards.

There also are two uphill holes, No. 5 and 18, which will put plenty of pressure on your game.

No. 5 (par 5, 576 yards from the back) has one of the most photographed tee boxes in Florida. An elevated tee, its sides are two huge flower beds and the front has green bushes cut to form the word "Innisbrook" in a bed of white flowers. You tee off over a lake to a fairway that slopes uphill. Pine trees line both sides of the fairway and bunkers crowd both sides of your landing area. Your second shot continues up the hill and the hole snakes left near the green, which is surrounded by bunkers.

Your drive on No. 18, a 432-yard par 4, has a more generous landing area for your tee shot, but there are nine bunkers lining the fairway and surrounding the green to make sure any wayward shot is duly penalized.

The par 5 No. 14 at Innisbrook's Copperhead Course is downhill, but the fairway and green slope toward the lake.

Region: Southwest

Address: P.O. Box 1088, Tarpon Springs

    (20 miles northwest of Tampa on Hwy. 19)

Phone: 813-942-2000

Access: Innisbrook resort guests only.

Yardage/Slope:

    Tournament: 7,087/140

    Championship: 6,536/132

    Middle: 6,149/125

    Forward: 5,506/128

Par: 36/35, 71

Green fees: $100 and up.

What the Panelists said:

Some of the best greens—in the best shape—that I've putted on in Florida. Big complex with two other outstanding courses." —Jim Williams (0).

"Innisbrook has long-standing experience and excellent reputation." —John Downs (1).

"Classic North Carolina-type course; beautiful." —Rafael Miguel (18).

"For a long, long time the top test of golf in Florida. Terrific resort; goes all out to please the golfer."—Will Frantz (0).

"Lots of elevation change, particularly for Florida. Great mix of holes." —Tom Stine (8).

"Beautiful course. Doesn't even look like Florida. Nice, quiet resort with fabulous amenities. First-class design." —Kevin Hayes (15).

3
PINE BARRENS
WORLD WOODS

Among those who love to golf, word of World Woods' existence spread in almost hushed tones, as if speaking too loud or too often about this paradise would spoil its charm and mystique.

The whispers sounded too good to be true: an unspoiled place, far from civilization, where 36 holes of golf in one day is the norm; where both courses are designed by Tom Fazio, the most prominent architect in the world today; where unlimited range balls and a three-hole warm-up course are all part of the deal (and so is the lunch).

Those who learn the way drive for hours—because it is more than an hour from any major Florida city—to see if the courses are as good as advertised. One of them, Pine Barrens, is so good that a national golf magazine compared it to venerable Pine Valley.

It received so much attention in late 1994 and 1995 that it is no longer a secret, but it is so far out of the way and in such a remote setting that you never feel crowded here.

Everything you may have heard about World Woods is true. And then some. Everything here is done on a grand scale. The driving range is huge—22 acres—and is shaped like a square so players can hit from all sides and practice shots with and against the wind. The target greens on the range even have sand bunkers so you can realistically practice approach shots.

The putting course is two acres and there is a nine-hole short course, seven par 3s and two par 4s, in case 36 holes of golf and three warm-up holes are not enough.

Pine Barrens may be Fazio's best public-access course in the country. The Pine Valley comparisons come because of the huge, unraked waste areas found on many of the holes.

"It happened to be a piece of land where cattle was raised," Fazio said. "About 20 years ago, it was planted with pine trees to protect the land from eroding. It was natural to create a sand-based course."

The natural-looking waste areas are dotted with tall, wild grasses. They serve as a sharp contrast to the immaculately manicured fairways and the square-shaped tee boxes.

There are also pine needles and rough that isn't too thick and fascinating golf holes with double fairways and incredible views. The elevated tees and greens give you panoramic views of the pine tree-lined fairways.

There is one area on the course —where the 4th, 5th and 15th holes are—where no trees were planted. "It happened to be a pasture area," Fazio said. "What do you do with an open pasture? We created a 'barrens' area, taking the sand out and using it elsewhere on the course."

No. 15, the shortest par 4 on the course, is among the most visually striking. The hole is only 330 yards from the elevated back tees. You must carry one massive waste bunker on your tee shot to one of two fairways separated by another huge waste area. Which fairway you go for depends on where the pin is located that day because you must carry that second waste area on your approach shot.

No. 15 is also one of only two holes with water. There is a small

No. 15

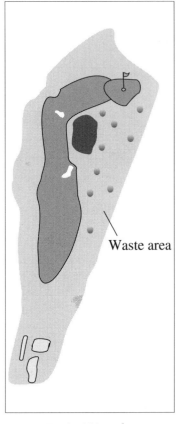

Par 4, 330 yards.

The rugged beauty of World Woods' Pines Barrens Course (No. 15 is pictured) make this Tom Fazio's most impressive work in Florida among public-access courses.

pond on the right side of the fairway, but it's only a factor if you really slice your tee shot or try to drive the green. On No. 3, a short par 3, your tee shot must carry the only other pond on the course.

Pine Barrens also features the finest collection of par 5s in Florida. Twisting and turning around waste areas to elevated greens, the holes do not demand distance as much as they demand club selection and shot location. On No. 4, for example, you must hit your drive and your approach shot over waste areas.

Your shots all require much thought and perfect execution, but when you birdie or par one of them, you feel like you have accomplished something. And that is what a great golf course is all about.

Pine Barrens' sister course, Rolling Oaks, is ranked No. 34. The course opened a temporary clubhouse in late 1994 and plans call for a permanent club house, a hotel and up to five more courses.

S C O R E C A R D

Region: Central

Address: 17590 Ponce DeLeon Blvd., Brooksville
(5 miles east of Hwy. 19 on State Road 98;
about 45 miles north of Tampa)

Phone: (904) 796-5500

Access: Open to the public.

Yardage/Slope:
Tournament: 6,902 yards / 140
Back: 6,458 yards / 134
Middle: 6,032 yards / 129
Forward: 5,301 yards / 132

Par: 36/35, 71

Green fees: $80 and up (for 36 holes, range balls).

What the Panelists said:

"An unusual course with a challenging layout." —Kevin Hayes (15).

"The best public course in the state; always in top condition."
—Kathy Lawrence (0).

"Best range I've ever seen." —Jim Witherspoon (4).

"One word to describe it—Radical! Enormous waste bunkers, lightning greens,
large landing areas." —Rafael Miguel (21).

"Great, great course and practice facilities." —Mick Elliott (18).

"Two fine courses, Pine Barrens especially. Best condition of any in Florida.
Feels like Pine Valley. Great fun." —Will Frantz (0)

"Great track.The No.1 facility in the state. Practice range No.1 in the country."
— Roscoe Staples (1)

"Best practice facility ever! Lack of clubhouse only complaint."
—Steve Melnyk (2)

4
BAY HILL CLUB

A true story: Arnold Palmer came to Orlando in 1965 to play an exhibition at a new Dick Wilson course. Palmer loved the course, probably in part because he shot a 66 that day. Five years later, Palmer put together a group of investors that bought the club.

Bay Hill, home of the PGA Tour stop that was called the Nestle Invitational, is now the winter home of Palmer. He has an office above the locker room, overlooking the course.

More than anything else, Bay Hill is a feeling. The place feels special, like time stood still in an era when golf was all that mattered. It feels like you might see Palmer stroll by at any minute.

It feels like you just joined a private club, which is what Bay Hill is; you can play the course only if you stay in one of the 59 rooms at the Lodge. You play golf in a place where playing golf is the important thing. That frenzy rush of daily-fee golf, that herd 'em out sensation of many resorts, is absent.

Just one great course (and an extra nine if you've got time to kill), draped in tradition and memories, something almost nonexistent in Florida.

Overall, the course is long and tough, but fair. The par 3s are all great, probably the best collection in Florida. And the three finishing holes are surpassed only by those at the TPC–Stadium Course.

And No. 18, though not as famous as the Doral Monster's No. 18, is significantly harder than that signature hole. If there is a break here, it is the par 5s, many of which are reachable in two. Most of the trouble on the par 5s is around the green, so if you play them smart, they are not as tough as the rest of the course.

Bay Hill begins with one of the toughest opening holes on the PGA Tour, a 441-yard monster (414 from the gold tees, 403 men's, 359 ladies) with three traps at the elbow of the fairway which turns slightly left 200 yards from the green.

No. 2 is the first of the four par 3s. This one is 218 yards from the back and plays downhill to a green that slopes severely from right to left.

No. 6 is a par 5 that defines the term risk/reward in golf. From the back tees to the center of the green is only 356 yards. About 350 of them are over water. The hole is boomerang-shaped around a lake that guards the entire left side. The question on your first two shots is simple: how much water do you want to cut off? The left side of the green is at the water's edge and two bunkers gobble up shots that stray right to avoid the water.

The signature No. 18 at Bay Hill has decided the fate of many Nestle Invitational tournaments, one of four PGA Tour stops in Florida.

But the course's real bite is on the back nine, where many tournaments are won and lost. Let's walk the last three holes:

No. 16, par 5 (481 yards, 452, 371): The tee shot is downhill, through a chute of trees, making this hole even shorter. Why then is this a good hole? Just play it. The length begs you to go for it, but the fairway is narrow and five traps line both sides just about where you want to land your tee shot. The fairway becomes a peninsula the last 120 yards before the green, with water on three sides, so laying up requires precision. To go for it also requires accuracy because water surrounds the front and left sides and bunkers line the back and right. Oh, and the green has three levels, so you need to hit the right tier.

No. 17, par 3 (219 yards, 182, 138): The green is situated the same way No. 12 at Augusta is, like the number 8 on its side. There are three tiers here also, and getting to the left side—where the pin is on tournament Sundays—is very tough. Hit it short and you are wet. Hit it long or left and you are in a bunker. Hit it right and you have a tortuous putt. No wonder this is one of the toughest par 3s on the PGA Tour each year.

No. 18, par 4 (441 yards, 414, 277): Simple golf equation: length + water in front of green = very tough hole. With apologies to Disney, this hole is the beauty and the beast. You must, without exception, nail your drive to have a prayer. Your second shot, with a middle to long iron, must carry a lake to a kidney-shaped green that hugs the water. The green sits low, the front lined with rocks. Behind the green, three huge bunkers at the bottom of mounds frame the hole. If the pin is to the right, the difference is two clubs.

No. 18

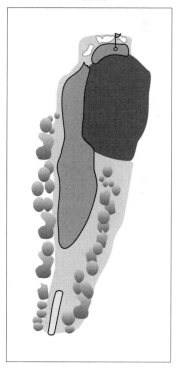

Par 4, 441 yards.

An example of how long this hole is: In the final round of the 1990 Nestle Invitational, Robert Gamez had 176 yards to the pin. He hit a 7-iron that went into the hole to beat—who else—Greg Norman and Larry Mize by one shot.

In 1991, Bay Hill was the site of Tiger Woods' first of three U.S. Junior Amateur victories. If you come during the winter, you just might see Arnie on the driving range. The place has that kind of feel.

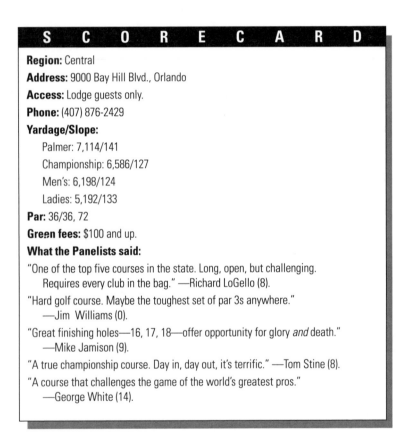

S C O R E C A R D

Region: Central

Address: 9000 Bay Hill Blvd., Orlando

Access: Lodge guests only.

Phone: (407) 876-2429

Yardage/Slope:

Palmer: 7,114/141

Championship: 6,586/127

Men's: 6,198/124

Ladies: 5,192/133

Par: 36/36, 72

Green fees: $100 and up.

What the Panelists said:

"One of the top five courses in the state. Long, open, but challenging. Requires every club in the bag." —Richard LoGello (8).

"Hard golf course. Maybe the toughest set of par 3s anywhere." —Jim Williams (0).

"Great finishing holes—16, 17, 18—offer opportunity for glory *and* death." —Mike Jamison (9).

"A true championship course. Day in, day out, it's terrific." —Tom Stine (8).

"A course that challenges the game of the world's greatest pros." —George White (14).

5
LONG POINT CLUB
AMELIA ISLAND PLANTATION

The prettiest course in Florida. No ands, if or buts. Some are tougher, some have more history. But none is prettier.

There are two back-to-back par 3s sitting on massive sand dunes next to the ocean. There are holes through the woods. There are trips through the swamps. And there are holes with great views of Nassau Sound.

"That was a fun and interesting site to work with," said Tom Fazio, who has three of his courses in the top 10. "We had the ocean to work with. And we had marsh, sand and vegetation. That is why we had two par 3s in a row on the ocean, because that is what fit."

That is the secret of Long Point. Everything fits. The course is nestled into the surroundings, not vice versa. It feels like you stumbled onto the course in the wilderness. "The location was so great that when the course opened, it looked as if it had been there for several years," Fazio said.

Amelia Island Plantation, one of the most secluded resorts in Florida, is tucked away on an island about 30 minutes northeast of Jacksonville, just south of the Florida–Georgia border. With two courses in the Top 20, it boasts 27 holes by Pete Dye and Fazio's 18 at Long Point. It is the most beautiful golf resort in Florida. Along with the Panhandle's Sandestin Resort in Destin, Amelia Island offers the best combination of great golf and a great beach.

Long Point is the only course in the Top 8 that does not host a PGA, LPGA or Senior PGA tour event. It ranks so high because of its setting and unique layout. Even driving to the resort is a treat. Highway A1A bisects the resort and huge moss-laden oak trees hang over the road.

Open only to Amelia Island Plantation resort guests, the course opened in 1987 and immediately drew rave reviews.

We'll start with the two famous holes, Nos. 6 and 7, the par 3s along the Atlantic Ocean. As you cross the road to the holes, a ranger

tells you what the wind is like and he
recommends how much club to take.
"The wind is starting to pick up a little," he told us when we played, a cold,
overcast day. "Take one more club than
you think you will need."

Standing on No. 6, 166 yards from
the back tees, you will see a stunning
view. Huge sand dunes on the right
drop toward the beach, the Atlantic
Ocean crashing in the background
about a 3-iron away. There is no room
for error here. The green sits on a little
knoll, the left side of the green dropping suddenly to a grass swale, two pot
bunkers on the right.

No. 7 is shorter at 158 yards, but
the green is smaller and more elevated.
There are no bunkers on this green,
but it is very tough to make it up and
down for par from the deep rough off
the green.

The rest of the course is just as
much fun to play. No. 2, a par 5 that doglegs left around marshland,
can be reached in two by long hitters if the drive hugs the left side of
the fairway. The fairway sits on a little plateau, with woods right and
marshland left just off the fairway. The green juts out into the marsh
like a peninsula, with trouble on both sides and behind the green.
The marsh extends back behind the green for several hundred yards
and provides a great view of Nassau Sound.

The front side is shorter and tighter than the back nine, which has
some long, tough carries over marsh and water. Like No. 11, a 424-
yard par 4 that requires a 224-yard carry off the tee over marshes. Or
like No. 13, a 438-yard, dogleg left par 4. To cut the corner, you must
hit it 263 yards! Fortunately, there is an alternate fairway down the
right side with a minimal carry for those less hardy.

Mostly the course rewards location over length. There is not much
room for wandering shots because the woods are thick and marshes
are not real easy to hit out of. Some of the greens will accept run-up
shots and most of the trouble on the course is lateral. On most holes

No. 6

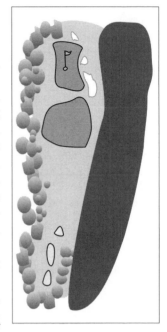

Par 3, 166 yards.

Tom Fazio's layout at Long Point (No. 6 is pictured) in Amelia Island is the most beautiful setting for public-access golf in Florida.

you have an option: you can go the short, hard way or play it safe and preserve a chance at par.

No. 15, a par 5 that tails right at the end, is a good example. Your tee shot must clear a small lake to a large landing area. If you stay right and hit it long, you can try to go for it in two, but you must carry another lake and a bunker that wraps around the right side between the green and the lake. You also can opt to go right around the lake, giving you a short iron approach on your third shot that takes the water almost completely out of play.

S C O R E C A R D

Region: Northeast

Address: Highway A1A South, Amelia Island
    (About 30 miles northeast of Jacksonville)

Phone: (904) 277-5907

Access: Amelia Island Plantation resort guests only.

Yardage/Slope:
    Championship: 6,775/127
    Regular: 6,068/121
    Intermediate: 5,539/119
    Forward: 4,927/120

Par: 36/36, 72

Green fees: $80 to $100.

What the Panelists said:

"A sleeper. A great challenge." —Steve Melnyk (2)

"Scenic, challenging and memorable as one of Fazio's best-designed courses. Set in the pristine marshes of Amelia Island. Be ready to be accurate and smart." —Barry Turnball (7).

"One of Tom Fazio's best designs. The two oceanside par 3s are terrific challenges when the predominant north wind is in the player's face." —Fred Seely (7).

"Scenic golf course. Part of Amelia Island Plantation so the amenities are outstanding." —Billy Varn (1).

"Classy Tom Fazio course at classy Amelia Island Plantation. Terrific use of the marshes. Can get lost in nature." —Chris Smith (12).

"Most beautiful setting in the area. Marsh, intracoastal and ocean setting. Some very tight fairways." —Charles Callahan (10).

"A great mix of long and short holes. Great par 3s on the ocean." —Don Green (1).

6
NORTH/SOUTH COURSE
GRAND CYPRESS RESORT

Of all the courses in the Top 10, the North/South Course is the most visually striking. It stuns your senses, this moonscape rising from the flattest land on earth. Forget about elevated greens—this is an elevated golf course.

There was a lot of talk—and not all good—about this course full of mounds and greens way up in the sky when it opened in 1984. Jack Nicklaus had been commissioned to design—create from nothing might be more accurate—this course as the cornerstone of a world-class resort. He didn't disappoint. This original 18-hole course, now part of a 45-hole complex, is as much fun to play as it is to look at.

The course has matured into one of Florida's best. It hosted an LPGA Tour event in 1994 and is always in immaculate shape. The once-unusual mounds that line the fairways are now commonplace. Look at Rees Jones' fine new design at LPGA International in Daytona Beach (No. 21 in Top 100).

Grand Cypress is one of the three best resorts in Florida (the others being Amelia Island Plantation and Innisbrook) and there is nothing better between Orlando and Miami. Everything is done first class. The resort's other layout, The New Course, is also a Jack Nicklaus design and the most unusual course in the state. It is ranked No. 20.

The clubhouse is my favorite in Florida. There is nothing better than an early morning breakfast in the comfortable dining room overlooking the huge double green where the North and South finishing holes meet. The walls of the clubhouse are littered with photographs of Greg Norman and several of the other pros who practice here.

The North/South and New courses provide a rare opportunity for you to play a Nicklaus course. Even though his headquarters are in Palm Beach, most of Nicklaus' courses in Florida are private. In fact, we haven't found any other Nicklaus courses in Florida that are public access.

The North/South Course requires you to keep the ball in play. If you don't, you will know it immediately.

Nicklaus framed the terraced fairways with moguls that define each hole. Your ball doesn't roll into the rough from the fairway, it rolls *off* the fairway and down to the rough—the epitome of target golf.

Tough elevated greens that usually are very fast make accuracy a premium over distance. There are very few opportunities to run it up to the green—hey, Jack never played that game, so you can bet his courses don't favor that shot. You have no choice here; you must hit the greens because there is no room for error.

A perfect example is No. 6 on the South, a long snaking par 5, 570 yards, with water left of the green. The green shoots up from the fairway like an upside teacup. Not only can you forget about trying to reach in two, but miss the green on your third shot and you are dead. A semi-circle green surrounds the right and back and moguls are on the left.

There is water everywhere, on the South par 3, a 158-yard carry to a bulkheaded green, all along the left side of the North's

No. 6

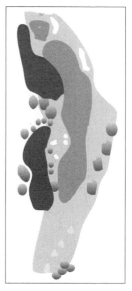

Par 5, 570 yards.

The small, elevated greens at Grand Cypress' North/South Course demand precise approach shots.

No. 3 (404 yards, par 4) and between the No. 9s on the North and South. The two holes run parallel to each other, both long par 4s, with a lake between them. They share a huge double green surrounded by huge mounds.

A third nine, the East Course, was built by Nicklaus and while not as famous as the North and South nines, it does have some excellent holes.

No. 5 is a 153-yard par 3 to an island green and No. 5 is a dogleg left par 5 around a lake. There are not as many moguls on the East and there is more room in front of the greens to allow for more bump and runs.

The golf school at Grand Cypress is one of the best in the state. Besides state-of-the-art equipment, there is a three-hole practice course, also designed by Nicklaus, for students to use.

There also are villas and a massive hotel, a golf school, equestrian center, seven restaurants, a huge lake with a sand beach and a croquet field.

S C O R E C A R D

Region: Central

Address: 1 North Jacaranda, Orlando

Phone: (407) 239-4700

Access: Grand Cypress resort guests only.

Yardage/Slope:

Gold: 6,993/130	Blue: 6,355/123
White: 5,823/121	Red: 5,328/119

Par: 36/36, 72

Green fees: $100 and up.

What the Panelists said:

"Fierce Nicklaus layout. Top-notch facility. Very severe design. Lotsa fun trying to shoot pars." —Will Frantz (0).

"Immaculate conditions. A five-star resort with outstanding customer service. Tournament conditions daily." —Jim Witherspoon (4).

"Silk from sow's ear. Flat, boring terrain turned into terrific golf course. Give Jack credit." —Tom Stine (8).

"Nice layout at a first-class resort. The course is challenging to a degree, but not impossible for an average golfer." —Kevin Hayes (15).

"Immaculate condition, beautiful facility; but there are some holes that are almost unplayable around the greens." —George White (14).

7
THE LINKS AT KEY BISCAYNE

Sometimes, not very often, great things happen in spite of efforts to the contrary. You can say that about hitting a 1-iron.

Or about municipal golf courses. Owned and operated by local governments, municipal courses often suffer from poor maintenance, nonexistent service, lack of interest or all three.

The best definition I ever heard for the woes of municipal courses came from a friend who, unfortunately, was talking about my swing. I had hit an awful tee shot and, exasperated, I turned to him and asked what I was doing wrong.

"A multiple of things too numerous to fix," he replied.

In Florida, there are two major exceptions to this description as applied to municipal courses: the Links of Key Biscayne and Eastwood Golf Club in Ft. Myers (No. 24). There are other exceptions, but these are the two where great things happened.

At Key Biscayne, it took, literally, an act of God.

Hurricane Andrew, in 1992, was the best thing that ever happened to the Links at Key Biscayne. In the aftermath of the hurricane, Dade County, which owns the course, used federal reconstruction money to bring back original architect Robert von Hagge and have the course renovated.

The result has been the best municipal course in the state. The service is sub-par and the clubhouse is woeful, but the course is nothing less than magnificent.

Key Biscayne is that once-in-a-great-while drive stored inside you, that wonderful blast, gently arcing from right to left, the one that, when you hit it, makes you fall in love with golf all over again.

Key Biscayne is a wealthy island town five minutes from downtown Miami. The golf course sits along one edge of the island, surrounded by mangroves and with stunning views of Biscayne Bay and the Miami skyline. There are no houses on the course and there never will be—the land was donated to the county on the condition it stays the way it is. Simply put, this is the best setting for a golf course in Southeast Florida.

The Miami skyline at the top is visible from the 18th fairway on the
Links at Key Biscayne.

It is the home of the PGA Senior Tour's Royal Caribbean Classic, held in early February. Original architect von Hagge, who also did all the Doral Resort courses and, not surprisingly, Eastwood Golf Course, redesigned the course in 1993. The greens are smaller, there are more bunkers and the course has a bolder look. "This is one of my favorite courses in Florida," von Hagge said.

His redesign gave the course a dramatic appearance: more undulating greens and large mounds around the greens. Some greens— such as the first one—were moved back. Bunkers were added around some greens and some obsolete fairway bunkers were removed.

The course got tougher, but most golfers love the course's new look.

From the first hole—a double dogleg par 5 that requires a drive over water and mangroves—to the last—another par 5, this one with water on both sides of the fairway—the course will test your accuracy and length.

No. 7

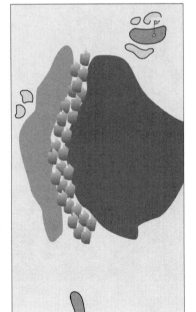

No. 3 is one of the best and most beautiful par 3s in Florida. The tee shot (187 yards from the back tees) shoots though a tunnel of mangroves over a small lagoon to a large green surrounded by bunkers.

No. 7 is one of the best—and toughest—par 4s (434 yards from the back tees) in the Southeast region. The hole is a dogleg right around a lake, with the green on the other side of the lake. Your tee shot must fade toward the lake to give you any chance of going for the green in two. The green is tough because it's shallow and wide, making it very difficult to

Par 4, 434 yards.

hold with the middle or long iron you must hit in order to reach it.

Amenities and service are the only drawbacks here. Key Biscayne is run by county government and the facilities make that painfully obvious: a small pro shop, a tiny locker room, a mediocre restaurant and haphazard service. But to the county's credit, the course is always in excellent shape.

Bottom line: what will impress you is an awesome golf course in an awesome setting, one that lets you walk most of the time.

S C O R E C A R D

Region: Southeast
Address: 6700 Crandon Blvd., Key Biscayne
Phone: (305) 361-9139
Access: Open to the public
Yardage/Slope:
   Blue: 7,070/138
   White: 6,389/129
   Red: 5,690/128
Par: 35/37, 72
Green fees: Under $50
What the Panelists said:

Stunning setting amid mangroves." —Joe Oglesby (15).

"The setting is marvelous. Panoramic views of Biscayne Bay and downtown Miami." —John Norton (2).

"South Florida's Pebble Beach. Great setting. Tough course. Too bad service and amenities aren't as good as the golf course." —David Wilson (13).

"Natural beauty like no other. Toughest first hole in Miami." —Ernie Rodriguez (15).

"One of the most beautiful courses in South Florida and equally as challenging." — Nat Moore (7).

"Gorgeous setting, incredible challenge, full of memorable holes." —Dave Sheinin (25).

"Great golf course with spectacular views." —Guy Boros (0).

8
BLUE COURSE
DORAL RESORT

The famed Blue Monster, as the storied course is best known, is in a state of flux. The most famous course in South Florida, at one of the country's most famous resorts, has had a roller-coaster career the past few years.

One of Dick Wilson's best designs, the course and resort enjoyed world recognition in the 1960s and '70s. Home to a PGA Tour event since 1962, the Blue Monster was consistently rated one of the Top 100 courses in the United States. But the Kaskel family, which owned the resort since it opened, let it slide in the 1980s.

In the early 1990s, some of the pros—most notably Greg Norman—began noting that the course had lost its bite. It fell off the lists of the top 100 courses. Architect Robert von Hagge, who designed the resort's other four courses and helped Wilson on the Blue Monster, asked the Kaskel family to let him refurbish the course.

The course was recently sold to KSL and the new ownership has begun a multi-million dollar facelift to the resort and the courses. PGA pro Raymond Floyd, who lives in South Florida, was hired to "put the teeth back into the Blue Monster." The Gold Course was closed down for much of 1995 and the Blue Monster will be closed for most of 1996.

Already, the signs of new ownership are being felt. The staff is nicer, the hotel rooms are being modernized and, most importantly, far greater attention and care are being paid to the courses. At the 1995 Doral–Ryder Open, pros and the media lauded the course's condition, saying it was in the best shape ever.

Floyd has said he will not change the course or any of the holes, but concentrate on restoring the original contours of the greens, which have lost some of their definition through the years.

There is no need for major changes. The course has some memorable holes, most notably No. 18, one of the best finishing holes in the country. Like the 18th at TPC–Stadium Course, there is water all along the left side. The hole is not as much of a dogleg left, but the water is definitely a factor on both the tee shot and the approach.

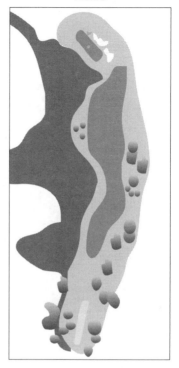

Par 4, 425 yards.

In the 1995 Doral–Ryder Open, Nick Faldo was leading on Sunday when he hit his drive into the water. Greg Norman, who followed and needed a par to force a playoff, pulled his approach shot into the water. And those were two of the best players in the world.

Why is it so tough? The 425-yard par 4 usually plays into the wind and the water lining the left side of the fairway makes it a treacherous driving hole. On the approach, the water pinches into the fairway in front of the green and hugs the right side.

But there are other great holes, including all the par 3s:

- No. 4—This is one of the toughest par 3s in Florida. It is 237 yards from the back tees and it seems to play longer because it is all carry over water to an elevated green. The green is huge and slopes severely from front to back. The wind is usually blowing across—to where the water is.

- No. 9—one of the best viewing spots during the Doral–Ryder Open—is a 163-yard carry over water that guards the front and left sides (guess where the pin is usually located). It plays into the prevailing wind.

- No. 13 has no water—for a change—and usually plays downwind, but it's 246 yards long (what do you think about hitting a driver on a par 3?); I've seen pros hit 1-irons and come up short.

- No. 15, at 174 yards, features an elevated green virtually surrounded by bunkers.

Among the par 5s, No. 8 is the best. The hole sweeps left, providing the closest thing to a blind tee shot on a flat course. The shallow,

At the famed Doral Blue Monster, No. 4 is one of the toughest par 3s in South Florida, requiring a long carry over water to an elevated green.

elevated green is guarded by water in the front. When there isn't much wind, players can go for it in two, but it is difficult to make the ball stay on the green.

Even the short holes are tricky. No. 11 is only 348 yards, but a massive bunker in the middle of the fairway makes the golfer choose left, right or over the top.

There are three other courses at the Doral Resort (from best to worst): Gold, Red and White. The course is open to the public. Guests staying at the resort get discounted green fees. Because of the ongoing renovations, make sure to call ahead to see which courses are open.

Doral also features a world-class spa, great practice facilities and one of the largest pro shops in the country. The pro shop has two floors of nothing but clothes, hats and balls. Interestingly, they don't sell golf clubs.

Region: Southeast

Address: 4400 NW 87th Ave., Miami

Phone: (305) 592-2000

Access: Open to the public; discount for resort guests

Yardage/slope:

6,939/127

6,597/125

5,786/124

Par: 36/36, 72

Green fees: $25 to $125

What the Panelists said:

"The course is getting a remake, but with slick greens and strong winds it remains a beautiful, lush monster."—Joe Oglesby (15).

"Blue Monster is still one of the best resorts in the world. The 18th hole will challenge any golfer."—Bill Rose (7).

"The course is usually in great condition and is fun to play."—Tracy Kerdyk (0).

"PGA Tour course with great history. Especially good because risk-reward for mid-handicappers from middle tees is very close to what the pros face." David Wilson (13).

9
BURNT PINE GOLF CLUB
SANDESTIN RESORT

The story about the origin of the course's name is almost as good as the golf course. The legend of Burnt Pine began when a Scottish sea captain, trying to outmaneuver the Union blockade during the Civil War, sailed into Choctawhatchee Bay during a severe thunderstorm.

The captain, carrying medical supplies to his brother in Mobile, ran aground in Horseshoe Bayou. Just then, lightning set a pine tree afire. Taking this as an omen, the captain abandoned his boat and buried his chest of gold at the foot of the burnt pine.

He then set out on foot to deliver the medicine. When he returned months later, he was stunned to find the whole area dotted with charred pine trees from a forest fire.

I am convinced it's under the burnt pine behind the 15th tee.

Anyway, the folks at Sandestin swear they didn't find it when they built Burnt Pine, the best course in Northwest Florida. Opened in late 1994, Burnt Pine Golf Club will not be a public treasure forever. Destined to be a private club, the course is open to guests of Sandestin Resort until the membership is full—or they find that chest of gold.

Rees Jones, who has gained national attention for his refurbishing of U.S. Open sites, has produced in Burnt Pine his best public-access work on Florida. This is not an easy task, considering two other new courses—LPGA International in Daytona Beach (No. 21) and Kissimmee's Falcon's Fire (No. 38), are first-rate courses.

At Burnt Pine, Jones has better land to work with and he did not disappoint in his goal: "We set out to build the best course in this part of the country."

Carved from a sandy pine forest and marshland, the course sits along Choctawatchee Bay, with three holes fronting the bay. "We had a wooded site that was framed in beautifully," Jones said. "The site has a seaside feel to it, with plenty of rolls, bumps, hollows and little cavities."

Burnt Pine is a course that grows on you with each hole. It is a peaceful place, where no one is hurried and the employees are called "hosts."

There is water or marshland on 12 of the holes and many of the greens are framed by the pine forest.

The course begins with a medium-length par 4 (404 yards, 355, 307) with a lake along the entire left side of the hole. Those bumps and hollows Jones described surface around the green.

Get your pars here early, because it gets tougher real quick. No. 4, at 444 yards from the back (420, 389), requires a big drive over wetlands. No. 5, a par 5 (532 yards, 491), has a lake along the left side of the hole and the green darts out to the left, bringing the water even more into play.

The real teeth of the course are on the back nine, during a three-hole stretch that is at the same time as tough and beautiful as any self-proclaimed Amen corner in Florida.

The 15th hole at Sandestin's Burnt Pine Golf Club, a new course designed by Rees Jones that includes panoramic views of the Choctawhatchee Bay.

No. 14

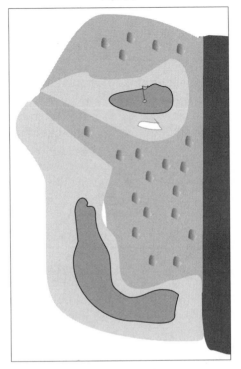

Par 3, 220 yards.

No. 13 is a long par 4 (433 yards, 408, 380) that doglegs right around a lake. The green sits low, with Choctawhatchee Bay as the backdrop. Your approach shot can be with almost any club, depending on the wind from the bay.

No. 14 may be the prettiest par 3 in Florida. To Jones' credit, he made it great by not doing too much to the land. Jones built a tee box and a green, both bulkheaded, and left the rest alone. Set along the bay, there are wetlands between the tree and green. It plays 212 yards from the back tees (193, 165), but, like on No. 13, the wind will dictate club selection.

"It's a big green, the biggest on the course," Jones said. "But it had to be because that's a do-or-die shot.

No. 15 is brutal. There is a tee box rising from the marsh set back against the Bay, which stretches this par 4 to 489 yards! It usually plays downwind, but from back there, your tee shot must carry more than 200 yards of marsh before the fairway even begins. Even from the next set of tees—413 yards—you need to crush your drive. Fortunately the fairway is the widest on the course. "That's a power hole," Jones said. "It was built that way to take advantage of the wind that generally will be behind you, blowing off the bay."

Two par 5s in the last three holes give you some hope, but you need to be careful—No. 16 has water along the entire right side and No. 18—at 577 yards—requires three good shots.

Sandestin Resort, which has the best beaches of any golf resort in Florida, has two other courses, Baytowne (No. 26) and Links (No. 58), ranked in the Top 100. Sandestin and Amelia Island Plantation are the two best golf/beach resorts in Florida for the entire family.

S C O R E C A R D

Region: Northwest

Address: 5500 Highway 98 East, Destin

    (Just east of Destin, between Pensacola and Panama City)

Phone: 904-267-6500

Access: Limited access to Sandestin Resort guests.

Yardage (Slope not available):

    1: 7,046

    2: 6,524

    3: 6,000

    4: 5,096

Green fees: Under $75.

What the Panelists said:

(Comments were limited because the course is so new)

"A superb new Rees Jones design. Routing and tees set up playability for golfers of all skill levels. Beautiful views on Choctawhatchee Bay, through wetlands and pines." —Ted Raymond (7).

"Resort golf with extraordinary attention to detail. Superior facilities, dining and accommodations with diverse activities for all family members." —W. Earl Daniel (4).

10
EMERALD DUNES

You know Palm Beach County is flat when one of the highest points in the county is the "SuperDune" at Emerald Dunes. The SuperDune, which is more than 50 feet high, is one of the many special touches here.

Emerald Dunes defines special touches. This is the facility that took the concept of upscale daily-fee golf and did it one better. There is a $2.5 million clubhouse, a fabulous Tom Fazio course, computers on every golf cart—and the SuperDune.

Three greens and three tees are incorporated into the SuperDune, a manmade mountain Fazio came up with. "Because we had a flat piece of land, we had to create something aesthetically pleasing and dramatic," Fazio said. "So we created a SuperDune."

The SuperDune has a waterfall behind the fifth green and houses the 18th tee, the start of one of the great golf holes in Florida. It also provides panoramic views of almost the entire course and the 60 acres of lakes.

The rest of the course is just as amazing. Its style is hard to describe, sort of a cross between a Scottish links course and a Carolina dunes course. There are lots of water and sand bunkers, but they are mostly used to enhance the aesthetic look of the course. Almost all of the water is lateral.

Emerald Dunes is the second partnership between Fazio and Raymond Finch, the club's president. Finch and Fazio collaborated on Wild Dunes, in Isle of Palms, South Carolina. Wild Dunes was rated one of America's 100 greatest courses by *Golf Digest* in 1995.

Emerald Dunes is among the most playable Fazio designs in the Top 50. There are few trees that come into play and it feels like the course is wide open. Don't be deceived. The greens are the best in South Florida. A couple of panelists, both single-digit handicappers, said that Emerald Dunes was a "hard par, easy bogey course." They meant the course was tough, but fair.

A good example is the par 5 5th, at 555 yards from the back tees. You need to hit three good shots to get around the massive lake running along the left side of the hole.

No. 9 is one of those great risk-reward holes. This par 4 has water all along the right side of the hole, begging you to try and cut off as much as you dare.

Even the tame-looking first hole is deceiving. A dogleg right, it looks like there is plenty of room to carry the bushes on the right side. But there is water and sand down there, making that a foolish risk.

Then there is No. 18, the 1990s version of a great finishing hole. It begins with the prettiest tee box in Florida. Perched high in the middle of the SuperDune, it has a rock creek meandering around it and it has a great view of the hole. Lush landscaping abounds. Along the right side, a long narrow bunker stretches from the base of the dune all the way to the green, separating the fairway from the lake. Dunes and bushes define the left side.

The hole is long, 436 yards from the back tees, and plays into the prevailing wind. The green is big and deep and there is no bunkers in front, giving you a change at running it on since you will be hitting a long iron or wood into it.

Emerald Dunes is expensive, but you get what you pay for. The course has become a favorite for some of Palm Beach's better players and was recently named the favorite course in Palm Beach by the 800 members of the Palm Beach County Golf Association. That is quite a coup considering there are 140 courses in Palm Beach County.

I asked Fazio, who designed four of the Top 11 courses in Florida, which course he would go play tomorrow if he could pick any of them. "It would be hard for me not to pick Emerald Dunes because it is one of those fun places to go play," he said. "It's a golfer's hangout."

No.18

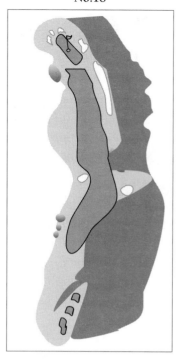

Par 4, 436 yards.

The finishing hole at Emerald Dunes starts from a massive dune that is an intergral part of several holes on this Tom Fazio layout.

S C O R E C A R D

Region: Southeast

Address: 2100 Emerald Dunes Dr., West Palm Beach

Phone: (407) 684-GOLF

Access: Open to the public.

Yardage/Slope:

Gold: 7,006/133	Blue: 6,558/129	White: 6,120/125
Green: 5,593/120	Red: 4,676/115	

Par: 36/36, 72

Green fees: $40-$125.

What the Panelists said:

"A Tom Fazio classic. Excellent use of a bland terrain." —Jim Warters (18).

"Great setting. A true golfer's golf course and facility." —Marty Martinez (0).

A superb Fazio design makes Emerald Dunes one of the most aesthetically pleasing courses one could hope to see. Always beautifully groomed. Multiple tee positions provides a very rewarding experience for golfers of any degree of proficiency." —Jim Montgomery (11).

11
PELICAN'S NEST

It is the little things Pelican's Nest does that make you fall in love with the place. Like ice-filled coolers in every cart. Like yardage books given to you free. Like free range balls, great summer rates and 36 great holes of Tom Fazio golf, which makes it tough to decide which 18 holes to play.

All this from a daily fee course. A big part of its charm is that you feel like you've discovered your own private club for the day. Pelican's Nest was among the first to offer superb service at a world-class daily fee course, a trend that other courses are copying with much success today.

This is not to detract from the excellent golf courses. Pelican's Nest is one of two facilities in the Top 50 course where 36 holes are considered as one entity. The other is Bluewater Bay Resort, No. 46. That's because there are four distinct nines here, and each one is just as good as the other. Fazio worked with what nature provided, snaking the course through mangroves and wetlands.

Almost all the tee boxes are islands carved out of the mangroves. There are no long carries over water or wetlands, but there are tight holes with little room for slices or hooks.

A highlight from each of the four nines:

Hurricane: No. 9 is a double dogleg par 5 (517 yards), with water along the entire left side of the hole and a lake about 250 yards out on the right side. Railroad ties line the fairway around the lake. The fairway narrows to a bottle neck in front of the green with bunkers stretching along both sides.

Gator: No. 9 is one of the toughest par 4s (434 yards) in Florida. It doglegs left at the end and you must hit a long, straight drive. Too far left and you can't see the green around the bend. Too far right and you have a long second shot over mangroves, over water, over a huge bunker to a shallow green that is surrounded by mangroves.

Seminole: No. 1 is a classic Fazio design. It is a sharp dogleg left (par 4, 390 yards); tall trees along the left prevent you from cutting off the corner. A huge bunker stretching across the entire fairway 100

No. 9 on the Hurricane Course at Pelican's Nest, a Tom Fazio gem just north of Naples and one of Florida's best maintained facilities.

yards out frame a small green. Oh, and water lines the entire right side of the hole, from tee to green.

Panther: No. 8 is my favorite hole here. A par 5 (526 yards) that requires more brain than brawn, the hole fades right toward a huge bunker that empties into a lake, resembling a beach more than a golf hole. The green is at a 90-degree right angle to the fairway, protected by the water. Bust your drive and you can go for it in two over the water. Otherwise, you can play up the fairway and take all the water and most of the sand out of play on your third shot.

S C O R E C A R D

Region: Southwest
Address: 4450 Pelican's Nest Dr., Bonita Springs
    (U.S. 41, 15 minutes north of Naples)
Phone: (813) 947-4600
Access: Open to the public
Yardage/Slope:

Hurricane
Championship: 3,458/139
Back: 3,220/131
Middle: 2,907/122
Forward: 2,511/119

Gator
Championship: 3,558/141
Back: 3,250/133
Middle: 3,103/127
Forward: 2,690/124

Seminole
Championship: 3,514/133
Back: 3,282/126
Middle: 3,025/120
Forward: 2,615/117

Panther
Championship: 3,461/133
Back: 3,246/127
Middle: 2,924/119
Forward: 2,534/122

Par: 36/36/36/36
Green fees: Under $75
What the Panelists said:
"This Tom Fazio course is simply the best. Each of the four nines is a challenge like no other. Once you start playing, you will want to play all 36."—Bill Janney (18).
"Always in top condition. Tight course, pristine setting, borders on too tight."
    —Mark Arrington (2).
"Excellent service, beautiful pro shop, great design, super condition."
    —Mike Clayton (0).

12
LAGOON LEGEND
MARRIOTT BAY POINT RESORT

Along the Emerald Coast, this course gets legendary status. When people tell you this is a tough course, for once they are not exaggerating. Lagoon Legend has the highest slope rating (152) of any course in Florida.

The reason is simple. There are so many do-or-die shots onto greens and no room for error off the fairways.

The course, designed by Bruce Devlin and Robert von Hagge (who also did Key Biscayne, No. 7), is less than 10 minutes from the Gulf of Mexico in Panama City Beach. It is one of two layouts (the other is Club Meadows, No. 100) at the resort.

Come then on a tour of the torture.

Your welcome is a dogleg right par 5, 542 yards. The fairway is among the most generous, but there is water in front and to the right of the green.

The second and third holes are monster par 4s, 405 and 450 yards each. The good news is there is no water on No. 3, but there are four bunkers surrounding the green.

The fourth is a par 3, but it's 208 yards and you must carry water the whole way. You finish the front with a par 4, 378 yards. You need to carry a bunker about 175 yards out and land on the fairway, which has water along the left. There is a small lake in front of the green and three bunkers behind it. Get the idea?

And that was the easy side.

The back nine is worse. There are tee boxes on the sides of lakes, an island green and an island fairway.

No. 10, par 4, 376 yards, is fascinating to play. Your tee shot must be perfectly placed with a long iron because the fairway ends 150 yards from the green, at a bunker. The green, a peninsula, is set off to the right, on the other side of a lake. Do-or-die approach, again.

The screws get turned tighter again at No. 13, ironically the shortest par 4 on the course. It is only 300 yards, but the island green sits in the middle of the swamp.

No. 14 is a long (434 yards) par 4 with a drive over a lake. How much of the water you cut off depends on how confident you feel. There is another lake to the right of the green and a 120-yards bunker on the right side of the fairway, between the lakes.

After a breather at No. 15, probably the easiest hole on the course, you get one of the best finishing trios this side of Bay Hill.

No. 16 is a par 3, 192 yards, over water to a bulkheaded green that is severely sloped from front to back. Two bunkers are behind the green in case you have thought of hitting long. The hole sits along the Bay, providing great views.

No. 17 is one of the toughest par 5s in Florida. A double dogleg (519 yards), it snakes through thick foliage down a narrow fairway. Your target off the tee is one of the three bunkers on the left side of the fairway. Your second shot is key here. You can cut off a little by staying left, but a lake along that side creeps into the fairway 133 yards from the green. Your approach must carry the lake to the green, which has five bunkers surrounding it.

No. 18 (par 4, 382 yards) is a great finishing hole. The hole is shaped like a boomerang. Your tee shot is out to an island fairway, where, as you can imagine, there is no room for error. You must hit it out long enough and far right enough to have a view of the green, which has water in front and to the right. A huge bunker sits behind the green.

Whew. I'm exhausted just remembering it.

S C O R E C A R D

Region: Northeast
Address: 100 Delwood Beach Road, Panama City Beach
Phone: (904) 235-6937
Access: Open to the public, discount for resort guests.
Yardage/Slope:
  Orange: 6,885/152
  Blue: 6,421/148
  White: 6,066/144
  Green: 5,559/135
  Red: 4,942/127
Par: 36/36, 72
Green fees: Under $75.

13

SAWGRASS COUNTRY CLUB
MARRIOTT AT SAWGRASS RESORT

This course is the answer to a good trivia question: where was the Players Championship held before it moved to the TPC–Stadium Course?

The course doesn't get the publicity of some of the other courses in the area, but among locals, this may be the favorite. The course has character, history, and, when the wind blows off the ocean, plenty of teeth.

Many panelists said this course was tougher than the TPC–Stadium when the wind blows. The club has three nines—East, West and South—but the East/West combination is the preferred 18 and the one used for the Players Championship.

Designed by Ed Seay, the course winds through marshland and lakes. Water comes into play on 14 of the 18 holes.

The East nine may be the toughest. Some highlights:

No. 2 (par 4, 394 yards) is a severe dogleg right with marshland on the right and in the middle of the fairway about 100 yards out.

No. 3 is par 3 to an island green of sorts—it is completely surrounded by bunkers.

No. 4 is a beautiful hole, a par 5 (501 yards) with a tight landing area for your tee shot. Your second shot is over a lake in the fairway and your third shot is to a small, elevated green atop a hill.

The fifth hole (par 4, 419 yards) is the best. You tee off high on a hill over water to a fairway bordered by marshes. The fairway bends right to a green tucked behind a lake and a bunker.

The last two holes on this side are monsters. No. 8 is a par 5 (524 yards) that zigzags along the edge of the lake running along the entire right side of the hole. There is a huge hollow between the tees and the start of the fairway. There is another hollow, though not as severe, in front of the green—which means your second shot should be back far enough to avoid a downhill lie for your third shot.

No. 9 is a bear of a par 4, 451 yards. The fairway is S-shaped, with the bulkheaded green at the top of the S. To have any prayer of reaching this green in two, you need to bust a drive that is long and doesn't reach the front end of the lake on the right side of the fairway.

The West nine is slightly easier, but all bets are off if the wind blows. The highlights here are Nos. 6 and 7. The first is a par 3, 198 yards, over water to a bulkheaded green and the latter is a par 4, 378 yards with water on both sides of the fairway and in front of the green.

S C O R E C A R D

Region: Northeast

Address: 10034 Golf Club Dr., Ponte Vedra Beach

Phone: (904) 273-3720

Access: Resort guests only

Yardage/Slope:

    Gold: 6,900/140

    Blue: 6,438/136

    White: 6,019/131

    Red: 5,128/119

Par: 36/36, 72

Green fees: $100 and up.

What the Panelists said:

"Excellent course. Very challenging when the wind is blowing off the ocean." —Billy Varn (1).

"Perhaps the toughest course in the area because of the wind from ocean and tight layout. A must play."—Charles Callahan (10).

"No. 1 in Jacksonville; possibly one of the top 10 hardest courses in the country when the wind is blowing."—Roscoe Staples (1).

14
WEST COURSE
GRENELEFE RESORT

It is longer than long. The West Course, the marquee attraction among the three courses at Grenelefe, is one of the longest in Florida—playing to 7,325 yards from the back tees.

Located about 30 minutes south of Orlando in Haines City, this Robert Trent Jones course has hosted the 1994 PGA Tour Qualifying School Finals as well as past U.S. Senior Open and Senior PGA qualifying events. In 1995, the West Course hosted sectional qualifying for the U.S. Open and the Florida Women's Amateur.

The course has everything tournament organizers want—length, elevation changes unusual for Central Florida, and fast greens. It is also the best maintained of the three courses at Grenelefe and has its own clubhouse and driving range.

Six of the 10 par 4s are more than 400 yards long, including the unreal 479-yard No. 14. Some holes are downhill, like the 564-yard par 5 fifth hole. But that one merely features a double dogleg to a

The hilly and curving holes on the West Course at Grenelefe (pictured is No. 5) feature small and fast greens.

well-bunkered green with a lake off to the left side. The lake, one of only two on the course, actually comes more into play on No. 6, a rare non-400 yard par 4s.

The other lake is at No. 17, a 405-yard par 4 that plays downhill. Problem is the hole turns left around the lake, which is at the bottom of the hill. This follows an impressive par 3 of 210 yards — straight uphill.

You get the picture. Fortunately there are four sets of tees: light green at 6,898 yards, whites at 6,199 yards and ladies at 5,398.

Grenelefe has two other good courses. The South Course (6,869 yards, par 71), designed by Ron Garl and Andy Bean, has huge greens, a little more water and some of Garl's trademark huge waste areas. It is ranked No. 94. The best holes are the double-dogleg par 5 eighth hole, with water on both sides of the fairway, and the 429-yard par 4 No. 17, with a carry over a huge waste area.

The East Course (6,802 yards, par 72), designed by Ed Seay, is the tightest of the three courses. Holes 12 through 14 are very good: a dogleg left par 5, followed by a beautiful par 3 over water and a downhill par 4 down a tree-lined fairway.

Grenelefe also features one of Central Florida's best tennis facilities, including two grass courts.

S C O R E C A R D

Region: Central
Address: 3200 S.R. 546, Haines City
Phone: (813) 422-7511
Access: Open to the public.
Yardage/Slope:

Championship: 7,325/130	Men: 6,898/126
Senior: 6,199/122	Ladies: 5,398/118

Par: 36/36, 72
Green fees: $50 to $99.
What the Panelists said:

"Tight, long and demanding. I've been playing the course since I was a kid and my game is still the same on this track." —Richard LoGello (8).

"Finest test in Florida. Pines, rolling terrain. Super 'rustic' resort." —Will Frantz (0).

"Could not be overrated. Smallish greens and long from the back tees. Great mix of long and short holes." —Jim Witherspoon (4).

15

CHAMPION COURSE

PGA NATIONAL

The course is named in honor of Jack Nicklaus, the champion who redesigned the Tom Fazio layout in 1990. The course starts out a little slow on the front nine, but picks up steam on the back nine and closes with the "Bear Trap."

The resort is the headquarters of the PGA of America. The Champion Course hosts the Senior PGA Championship and many tournaments have been won and lost on those last four holes. Nicklaus added some mounding and contours in his redesign, but most of his work was on the greens and the back nine. Water comes into play on 16 holes, including the final four.

The best hole on the front side is No. 8, a long par 4 (422 yards). This is the best driving hole, with an ample fairway. You need a good drive, because your approach must carry the edge of a lake that cuts into the fairway and make it up to the elevated green.

The back nine has more variety. No. 10, a straight-away par 5, is the only hole on the back with no water, so get your birdie or par here. It immediately gets tougher, with the No. 1 handicap hole next. At 444 yards from the back, No. 11 requires that you hit a good drive to have any chance. The green is fronted by water, so you have to airmail the approach to a kidney-shaped green.

The real fun (or pain) begins on No. 15, the start of the "Bear Trap." The 179-yard par 3 has water right of the green and a big bunker left of the green. Raymond Floyd put two balls in the water here during the final round of the 1994 Senior PGA Championship to lose the tournament to Lee Trevino.

No. 16 is a par 4 (432 yards) that sweeps right around a lake. A long bunker between the lake and the fairway further narrows your landing area. When the prevailing wind blows in your face, the hole gets tougher. The green has water on the right, where a greenside bunker also sits. The green has two tiers and slopes toward the water.

No. 17 is an even harder par 3 than No. 15, if that is possible. A virtual island green, it is shorter at 166 yards, but usually plays into the wind. There is no good spot to bail out. There is room behind the green, but it is a knoll and if you land there, you're faced with chipping down to the green and toward the water.

You finish with a par 5 (545 yards) dotted with a dozen bunkers, most of them on the left side. On your tee shot, pick one of the bunkers you think you can carry and fire away. Your second shot needs to draw back toward the bunkers, because a lake borders the right side.

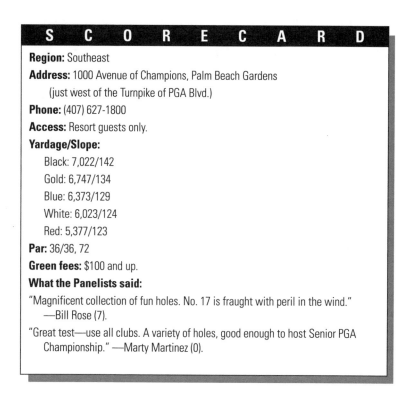

S C O R E C A R D

Region: Southeast

Address: 1000 Avenue of Champions, Palm Beach Gardens
(just west of the Turnpike of PGA Blvd.)

Phone: (407) 627-1800

Access: Resort guests only.

Yardage/Slope:

Black: 7,022/142

Gold: 6,747/134

Blue: 6,373/129

White: 6,023/124

Red: 5,377/123

Par: 36/36, 72

Green fees: $100 and up.

What the Panelists said:

"Magnificent collection of fun holes. No. 17 is fraught with peril in the wind."
—Bill Rose (7).

"Great test—use all clubs. A variety of holes, good enough to host Senior PGA Championship." —Marty Martinez (0).

16
AMELIA LINKS
AMELIA ISLAND PLANTATION

Before Pete Dye moved down the road to build the famous TPC–Stadium Course, he designed the original 27 holes for this resort. Tom Fazio would come later with Long Point (No. 5), giving Amelia Island two of the Top 20 courses in Florida.

Dye put together three very different nines—Oakmarsh, Oysterbay and Oceanside. Each has its own character and charm.

Oakmarsh is the longest, and not surprisingly, the toughest. Dye redesigned it in 1989, making it more defined. Oysterbay has forced carries over marshland on four holes, including the last three. Oceanside has, what else, three holes in a row along the Atlantic Ocean, the closest you can get to Pebble Beach without leaving the state.

There is one common thread woven through the three nines—hit your long irons well. Length is not a problem here. The Oysterbay and Oakmarsh combine for 6,502 yards from the championship tees. The problem is keeping the ball in play. The fairways are tight and the greens are small. The good news: the greens are relatively easy to putt; Long Point's greens are much tougher.

A quick round around the three nines:

Oakmarsh can be defined by No. 3, a short par 4 (317 yards), with oak trees lining both sides of the sliver that is the fairway. A bunker 200 yards from the tee reduces the fairway to 20 yards across. A single tall pine tree behind the bunker makes carrying the bunker very, very tough. If you go too far left, the trees block your view of the green, which has two bunkers in front.

No. 8 is a short par 4 (342 yards), but water replaces trees as the trouble. You tee off across a tidal creek to a fairway bulkheaded all along the right side. Your approach is back over the tidal creek to a small elevated green bulkheaded in front.

The tee shot on No. 8 at Oysterbay is the most dramatic at Amelia Links. To your left, rivers snake through the marshland, which wraps around the tee box and extends about 190 yards in front of you and then all along the left side of the hole.

It is the longest par 4, at 441 yards. Once you clear the marsh, the hole curls left slightly, around the marsh, making your second shot a bear.

While the Oakmarsh-Oysterbay combination has hosted several high-profile tournaments, including the U.S. Women's Mid-Amateur, the Oceanside draws most of the attention from the resort's guests. It is very rare that you can play three holes along the Atlantic Ocean. Oceanside has a more rugged look and is the nine that most resembles the traditional links style.

The three ocean holes—4, 5 and 6—sit atop mammoth dunes, some as high as 60 feet. You get great views of the Atlantic and the unique opportunity to play golf on one of the most expensive pieces of real estate in Florida.

No. 4 is a 342-yard par 4 and Nos. 5 and 6 are back-to-back par 3s. No. 5 is shorter (133 yards), but the green is elevated and two bunkers on the right are tough to get over when the pin is back and the wind is blowing.

No. 6 is a long par 3 (178 yards) and is the only hole on the course with no bunkers. The trick for these three holes is figuring out which club to use when the wind is blowing, which is almost always.

S C O R E C A R D

Region: Northeast
Address: Highway A1A South, Amelia Island
Phone: (800) 874-6878
Access: Resort guests only.
Yardage:

Oakmarsh	Oysterbay	Oceanside
Championship: 3,308	Championship: 3,194	Championship: 2,832
Regular: 2,978	Regular: 2,832/	Regular: 2,532
Intermediate: 2,798	Intermediate: 2,723	Intermediate: 2,388
Forward: 2,560	Forward: 2,498	Forward: 2,231

Par: 36/36/36
Green fees: $65–$85.
What the Panelists said:

"Fun and not overbearing." —Steve Melnyk (2).

"Without a doubt the most well-maintained golf course you might ever play."
    —Barry Adeeb (8).

"Golf in a very natural setting." —Mary Hafeman (0).

17
GOLDEN OCALA

I first heard of Golden Ocala from Earl Grey, the former superintendent of Key Biscayne (No. 7) and now with the Golf Club of Miami (No. 29). Grey, one of the quietest and most reserved people you'll ever meet, spoke of this place like a kid describing the best Christmas present he ever got.

Grey, who has been in the golf ownership business on the west coast of Florida and in partnership with Raymond Floyd, fell in love with Golden Ocala when he saw it. He was so impressed that he got Floyd to come up and see it, because the course was up for sale. They bid on the course, which has changed ownership several times. They were outbid by foreign investors.

Golden Ocala has 10 holes designed by Ron Garl and eight replica holes, patterned after famous holes from around the world. "The two Augusta holes are exact replicas," Grey insisted. Frankly, I didn't believe him.

I stopped at Golden Ocala on the way to the Masters tournament. I saw both courses within 24 hours of each other. Golden Ocala's replicas of Augusta's No. 12 and 13 are amazing, down to the azaleas behind the par 3 green and the downhill par 5 No. 13. It was eerie.

There are also copies of St. Andrews' No. 1 and 17 (the Road Hole), Baltusrol's No. 4, Royal Troon No. 8 (the Postage Stamp), Muirfield No. 9 and No. 16 at Augusta. The Royal Troon hole is the other great copy with the elevated tee and the really elevated green.

The other 10 holes are just as good. The rolling fairways wind through a thick pine forest. The greens are all framed beautifully by the tall pine trees. There are no parallel fairways and No. 9 is about as far from the clubhouse as you can get.

No. 1 is a majestic par 5 (541 yards) through towering pines that turns left at the end to a slightly elevated green. The second hole is a 377-yard par 4 that seems to have more sand than fairway (this is Garl design, remember). There's a huge bunker to drive over on the tee shot and then your approach is over a massive U-shaped bunker in front and around the green.

No. 5—the Augusta No. 12 copy—begins a string of five replica holes. The last three holes on the course are the other three replica holes, ending with a copy of Augusta's No. 16, a par 3 over water.

Golden Ocala's amazing forest setting—there are no houses anywhere on the course—and fine variety of holes make up for the pedestrian clubhouse and disappointing service. But like Key Biscayne, you come here when you want to play golf. If you want service and plush clubhouses, go somewhere else.

S C O R E C A R D

Region: Central

Address: 7300 U.S. Hwy. 27, Ocala
(3 miles west of I-75, exit No. 70)

Phone: (904) 622-1098

Access: Open to the public

Yardage/Slope:
Blue: 6,735/132
White: 6,197/124
Red: 5,595/124

Par: 36/36, 72

Green fees: Under $50.

What the Panelists said:

"Lacks some amenities that the others have, but ranks with them as a test of golf. Might have more memorable holes than any course in Florida."
—Jim Williams (0).

"Replica holes are very good. Very picturesque, beautiful trees."
—Kathy Lawrence (0).

"The replica holes are interspersed throughout the course, with the remaining holes more than holding their own for a most enjoyable golfing experience."
—Jim Montgomery (11).

18
OSPREY RIDGE
WALT DISNEY WORLD

The fact that Osprey Ridge exists at all, let alone that Tom Fazio was hired to design it, is the most concrete proof available on the golf boom in Florida. Osprey Ridge, which opened at the same as the Pete Dye-designed Eagle Pines (No. 53), brought to 99 the number of golf holes at Walt Disney World. Disney is as committed to golf as it is to that little black mouse.

Word is Disney is not done. Look for Robert Trent Jones Jr. to join the list of world-class architects to design a Disney course. For now, Osprey Ridge is the best of the six courses.

Set in an isolated tropical wilderness, Osprey Ridge is one of the more wide-open Fazio courses. Osprey Ridge and Eagle Pines share a clubhouse, Bonnet Creek, and are adjacent to each other just northeast of Epcot Center.

The best way to describe Osprey Ridge is that it is like Pine Barrens' little brother: they look a lot alike, but one looks much bigger. Both have the elevation changes and unique dramatic holes.

Osprey Ridge is a fun course to play. It is not overbearing, but demands good shots. The course is immaculate, the setting peaceful and there is that classic Disney service.

Water comes into play on only eight holes, but four of the last five holes. There is everything you would want: two great par 3s, two tough par 5s and a great finishing hole.

The par 3s: No. 3 (193 yards) is my favorite hole on the course. The tee sits high on a plateau and you hit over a valley to an elevated green that is shallow and wide. You need to hit it high to hold the green. No bunkers, no gimmicks, just a beautiful hole, you and one swing.

No. 17 is longer—217 yards—and tougher. From an elevated tee, you hit to a low-lying green with water in front and left. The side of the green bordering the water is rock-lined and there is a ridge in the middle of the green.

The par 5s: No. 9 (510 yards) forces you to pick between what you think you can do and what you know you can do. The hole doglegs right around a lake and because it isn't too long, you can try and stay right, flirting with the water in an effort to get home in two. The same debate rages on your second shot.

No. 16 (542 yards) is a three-shot hole and the key here is the second shot. The landing area for the tee shot is the most generous on the course. The hole turns almost 90 degrees left the last 120 yards and a lake on the left creeps in and reduces the fairway where you want to land your second shot.

The finishing hole: A beastly par 4 at 454 yards, the hole snakes right around a river. Three huge bunkers in a row—they look more like the beach, because they front the river—make the idea of reducing the yardage by staying right a foolish venture. The green is long and narrow, so you can conceivably run it on, but it would be like trying to run a golf ball down the street and expecting it to stay on the road.

S C O R E C A R D

Region: Central

Address: 3451 Golf View, Lake Buena Vista
   (On Walt Disney World property)

Phone: (407) 824-2270

Access: Open to the public; discount for Walt Disney World resort guests.

Yardage/Slope:
   Talon: 7,101/135
   Crest: 6,680/128
   Wings: 6,103/121
   Feathers: 5,402/124

Par: 36/36, 72

Green fees: $40 to $100.

What the Panelists said:

"First class resort and a nice golf course. Course is not overly difficult. Good atmosphere."—Kevin Hayes (15).

"A nature-lover's delight: wild animals, birds and a course that is a work of art. No. 18 requires two long, precise shots."—Bill Rose (7).

"It's always perfect. You never see a maintenance person. It's almost like elves do it."—Paige Phillips (0).

19
GOLF CLUB OF AMELIA ISLAND

The least famous of the courses at Amelia Island, the Golf Club of Amelia Island, is famous in Northeast Florida for its great setting and superb conditioning. Formerly named the Summer Beach Golf Club, the course is accessible to guests of the Summer Beach Resort and the Ritz-Carlton.

The Ritz-Carlton provides a majestic backdrop on many of the holes, the way the historic Biltmore Hotel in Coral Gables oversees its golf course (No. 50).

Designed by PGA Tour veterans Mark McCumber and Gene Littler, the course is really two courses in one. The front side meanders through oak hammocks and tall pines. The back nine has more ponds and marshes.

The local panelists continually rave about the course's conditioning, which is saying something because the Northeast Florida region consistently has the best maintained courses in the state. It is a point of pride and golfers have come to expect great conditions on the golf courses.

The fairways are tight, with thick vegetation lining many holes and especially around the greens. The greens here are huge and several are more than 10,000 square feet (you could build a huge house on some of them and have room for a swing set in the backyard!).

When you're not trying to stay out of the woods, you're trying to stay out of the water and/or the marshland. On No. 6, a par 5, you need to hit over marshland three times to get to the elevated green protected by a massive, 10-feet-tall bunker with an open face.

The inclusion of Golf Club of Amelia Island in the Top 20 means there are three courses from the same small barrier island in the Top 20, the best collection of courses anywhere in the state (the others are Long Point at No.5 and Amelia Links at No. 16).

The Club is also home to the Swing Dynamics Institute, which teaches principles based on how the mind and body work together to build a sound swing.

S C O R E C A R D

Region: Northeast

Address: 4700 Amelia Island Parkway, Amelia Island

Phone: (904) 277-8015

Access: Guests of the Ritz-Carlton and Summer Beach Resort

Yardage/Slope:

Championship: 6,681/127

Regular: 6,119/124

Senior: 5,741/120

Ladies: 5,039/122

Par: 36/36, 72

Green fees: $50–$100

What the Panelists said:

"Great greens and the Ritz on the ocean. What could be better?" —Pat Paolini (16).

"One of the best conditioned courses in the area; greens are always in great shape. Risk/reward factor on many holes." —Charles Callahan (10).

20
NEW COURSE
GRAND CYPRESS RESORT

This is a course unlike anything you have seen in Florida. There are no trees, no rough and very little water. It looks as if you are playing in a large meadow—with 145 bunkers thrown in to keep your attention.

There are seven double greens. There is a stone wall lining one fairway and another one behind, yes, the 17th green. If it conjures up images of Scottish courses, that's the intent.

Designed by Jack Nicklaus, the New Course tried very hard to duplicate many of the holes at legendary St. Andrews. There are even photographs of the original holes next to some tee boxes so you can see for yourself how close Nicklaus came.

First you must get over the initial shock of the course's appearance—the first and 18th fairways are not only parallel, there is nothing—not even rough—separating them. The fairway looks wider than it does long.

You get used to it pretty quickly and the course becomes a lot of fun to play. At 6,773 yards from the back tees, length is not the issue here, accuracy is. There are pot bunkers in the fairways—some as deep as 12 feet and many with ladders in them—and split-level landing areas which require lots of thought.

Two of the par 5s, the best holes on the course, illustrate the point. No. 6 is a dogleg left of only 496 yards. The left side of the fairway is the lower and shorter route, but it is less even. The right side is higher and more level, providing the best angle into a green protected by four pot bunkers.

But No. 15 (570 yards), the signature hole, is even more fun. A stone wall lines the right side of the fairway. Behind it, the only lake which comes into play. The fairway itself has two tiers. If you hit it long, you can try and fly the four pot bunkers in the middle of the fairway, 235 yards out. If not, you can go for the lower left tier of the fairway.

The pot bunkers—complete with ladders—give The New Course at Grand Cypress that unmistakable Scottish feel.

The fun isn't over yet. A massive bunker, stretching almost the entire width of the fairway and up to 30 yards deep, sits about 100 yards in front of the green. Your lay-up can be short in front of the trap or you can try and carry it to leave yourself a sand wedge into a huge double green.

S C O R E C A R D

Region: Central
Address: 1 North Jacaranda, Orlando
Phone: (407) 239-4700
Access: Grand Cypress resort guests only.
Yardage/Slope:
   Blue: 6,773/126   White: 6,181/117   Red: 5,314/117
Par: 36/36, 72
Green fees: $100 and up.
What the Panelists said:
"Unique design: deep pot bunkers, well maintained." —Jim Hall (10).
"Very unique." —Mike Jamison (9).
"Every hole is fun to play; every hole is a delight to study." —Bill Rose (7).

21

LPGA INTERNATIONAL

When the LPGA relocated its national headquarters from Texas to Daytona Beach in 1989, it was the start of an extensive effort to create a first-class resort, plus residential and commercial development to surround its headquarters.

LPGA International, the first of two courses to be built on the site just west of I-4 and the Daytona Speedway, is an impressive debut. Built as the permanent home to one of the LPGA's richest tournament, the Spring Championship, the course is one of the first in the country built specifically for professional women golfers.

Consider it the LPGA's version of the TPC at Sawgrass. Architect Rees Jones, who has been hired to tune up the classic Pinehurst No. 2 for the 1999 U.S. Open, designed LPGA International by starting with the middle tees and working out. This is not to say the course is short—it plays to 7,088 yards from the black tees—or easy—there is water or wetlands on every hole, including carries on two par 3s.

But with six sets of tees (including 6,664 yards from the blue tees, 6,225 from the whites), the course sets up well for golfers of all levels.

The fairways are framed with mounds that break up the flatness of the area as well as serving for prime viewing spots for spectators during the tournament. At first glance, this appears to be an easy course. There are few trees, the course is wide open and the greens are large.

Then you start playing. The greens are really two and three greens in one, divided by sections and mounds that require precise approach shots. The water and wetlands lining many of the fairways and surrounding some of the greens make you think about the best approach. And when the wind blows, the course is as tough as any in Florida.

The par threes are all excellent, especially No. 6 and 17, with water fronting the green. No. 16 is a beautiful par 5 with water on the left side and a tough, elevated green.

The facility features three practice holes, three putting greens, two chipping greens, and a grass driving range. There is more to come. Arthur Hills will design a second golf course and a 450-room hotel is planned, as are residences.

S C O R E C A R D

Region: Northeast

Address: 300 Champions Dr., Daytona Beach

Phone: (904) 274-3880

Access: Open to the public.

Yardage: 7,088–5,744

Par: 36/36, 72

Green fees: $25 to $60

What the Panelists said:

"Upcoming facility . . . Condition is superb; Best greens in Volusia County."
—Kathy Lawrence (0).

"New course and in great shape . . . Exceptional practice facilities that feature
three practice holes—a par 3, 4 and 5." —Ken Willis (15).

22
TPC–TAMPA BAY

Once the TPC–Stadium Course became a hit with spectators and golfers in the 1980s, the PGA Tour went into the golf course business, designing a handful of TPC courses throughout the country. Many of those became very successful and the PGA Tour continued building and managing golf courses.

Architect Bobby Weed, who helped out on the two TPC courses at Sawgrass, designed several of the PGA Tour's new projects. Weed designed the Golf Club of Jacksonville (No. 80) and all three courses at the Golf Club of Miami (No. 29).

Weed, with Chi Chi Rodriguez serving as the player consultant, designed the TPC at Tampa Bay. It is now home to the GTE Suncoast Classic, a Senior PGA Tour event.

The so-called "Stadium Golf" design, though popular, will not continue to multiply. The PGA Tour, for economic reasons, has curtailed its forays into public golf.

TPC–Tampa Bay gives you a chance to play where the pros play. The course is wide open and not overly long (the Senior Tour plays here, remember!). The best part of the course is the greens. They are fast and always in good shape. Most are slightly elevated; they don't sit up high, but the edges drop off sharply, mostly into grass swales.

Just as the Senior players do, the key is not to hit it long here, but to be accurate. And to play on days when the wind doesn't blow. There is nothing to stop the wind out here and when it gets going, hitting and holding the fast greens becomes very tough.

The course is mostly flat and most of the challenge comes from the water all over the place. The first hole, for example, is a dogleg right par 4. Any kind of drive that doesn't drift right will get you past the corner. The green is crowned and surrounded by a grass swale and bunkers all around.

The only surprising element about the TPC–Tampa Bay is the lack of a clubhouse. There is one trailer for the pro shop and another for the snack shop.

S C O R E C A R D

Region: Southwest

Address: 5100 Terrain de Golf Dr., Lutz

Phone: (813) 671-3311

Access: Open to the public.

Yardage: 6,898–6,008.

Par: 36/35, 71

Green fees: $50 to $100.

What the Panelists said:

"A gifted design; course needs better management." —John B. Downs (1).

"Course is in excellent condition; excellent layout. No clubhouse." —Bob Harig (16).

"Challenging, fast greens. Secluded. No. 18 is a long, tough par 4."
    —Rafael Miguel (21.

23
BLOOMINGDALE GOLFERS CLUB

Everything you need to know about Bloomingdale: The day I played there, LPGA player Vicki Goetze was playing. It was a Saturday and she had just missed the cut at the Sprint Championships on the other side of the state. Goetze, Colleen Walker and PGA pro Lee Janzen all have their own parking space here.

They come for the golf course, a wonderful layout with a serene setting that attracts many of the area's best players. More than 200 of the members have single-digit handicaps.

Bloomingdale is golf in a very natural setting. Half of the course's property is designated a wildlife preserve. Winding through old oaks, tall pines, ponds and marshes, the course is as wonderful to look at as it is to play.

The phrase "tough but fair" has become a cliché (and you will not see it anywhere else in this book), but if ever a course defined that phrase, this is it.

There are many areas where the vegetation lining the fairways is so thick you will never find a ball, but you never feel crowded. There is a lot of water on 14 holes—but you never feel you are drowning.

No. 1 (par 4, 385 yards) is a good example. At the tee there is water to the right and in front and forest to the left. But you can clear the water with a long iron and still have a middle to low iron into a good-sized green that has water protecting the right side.

You will need all kinds of shots here. Nos 2 and 6 are long par 4s that call for a draw off the tee. Nos. 4 (a par 5) and 5 (a par 4) require a fade to take full advantage of the holes' layout.

There are also some great risk/reward holes, No. 9 being the best of them. It is a double dogleg par 5 (546 yards). If you hit a long fade around the first corner you can try to carry the lake in front of the bulkheaded green and go for it in two. If not, your second shot must be a precise one to an island fairway that has marsh in front and back, and water left and right.

The raccoon is the logo at Bloomingdale (pictured is the par 5 No. 9), where animals share the course with golfers.

Goetze hit a good drive that day I saw her there, but she decided to play it safe and hit it to about 100 yards short of the green. One of the men she was playing with was a little in front of her and he went for it in two, landing in the back of the green.

Like all good golf courses, Bloomingdale has a strong trio of finishing holes. No. 16 is a par 5 that turns right at the end, has water on the right and lots of bunkers as you get close to the green.

No. 17 is the best par 3 on the course, 206 yards over water to a bulkheaded green. There is no room for error here.

No. 18 is a severe dogleg left par 4 (409 yards) with a carry over marshland to a large green. This is a beautiful hole with tall trees lining both sides of the fairway.

S C O R E C A R D

Region: Southwest

Address: 1802 Nature's Way Blvd., Valrico

Phone: (813) 685-4105

Access: Open to the public Monday through Thursday and Friday until noon.

Yardage: 7,165–5,506

Par: 36/36, 72

Green fees: $50–$75

What the Panelists said:

"A difficult test. Where the top pros in the area play." —Bob Harig (16).

"Super practice facility. Great layout." —Mike Clayton (0).

"This course is very serene, with animals everywhere. Good test of golf; in immaculate condition." —Kevin Hayes (15).

24
EASTWOOD GOLF CLUB
(FT. MYERS)

When I asked architect Robert von Hagge to give me his rankings of the courses he designed in Florida, he listed Eastwood second to only Key Biscayne (No. 7 in this book). What was really interesting were the two courses listed right below Eastwood—classics such as Doral's Blue Monster and Bay Hill (both Top 10 courses in this book).

Eastwood and Key Biscayne are the only municipal courses in the Top 25. But unlike Key Biscayne, which has poor service and no real clubhouse, Eastwood has excellent service and a good clubhouse.

But like Key Biscayne, Eastwood's greatest charm is its setting. Eastwood, owned and operated by the city of Ft. Myers, is in an isolated, wooded park setting. There are towering pine trees and lots of water.

A nature center behind the course attracts much of the wildlife to the area, and much of it wanders through Eastwood. The course rolls through the forest, the dense trees broken up by ponds and lakes, usually around the greens. Eastwood is also the cheapest course in the Top 50, and summer green and cart fees are under $20 on weekends.

Besides its fine setting, Eastwood is very well maintained and proof that municipal courses can compete with the high-priced daily fee courses for accolades if management pays attention to course conditions.

At Eastwood, the challenge is to stay out of the forest and the water. It can be tough. No. 10 is a 413-yard par 4 that has a 200-yard carry over water off the tee. The hole then turns left around trees to the green.

No. 18 is a straight-away par 4, except there is water in front of the elevated green and trees all along the right side.

Eastwood used to be one of the great secrets in Southwest Florida—the course does almost no advertising—but *Golf Digest* has ranked it as one of the top 50 public courses in the United States for the past eight years. It is now well-known, but still inexpensive and not overly crowded.

S C O R E C A R D

Region: Southwest

Address: 4600 Bruce Herd Lane, Ft. Myers

Phone: (813) 275-4848

Access: Open to the public.

Yardage: 6,772–5,116

Par: 36/36, 72

Green fees: Under $40.

What the Panelists said:

"Well worth playing. Rated one of the nation' s best public courses."
—Bill Kilpatrick (10).

"Pure golf, no home sites. Not overly long, but demanding. Has gotten better each year." —Doug Oselett (10).

"Fair test of golf, good mix of hole difficulty. You will hit all clubs during a round."
—Mark Arrington (2).

25
SOUTH COURSE
TURNBERRY ISLE RESORT & CLUB

This is a classic course, designed by a classic architect, located in a classic resort. Everything here is class, from the valet parking to the underground cart storage (no unsightly cart barn) to the deluxe resort accommodations.

A Robert Trent Jones design, the course has steadily improved each year for the past decade. Raymond Floyd, who lives nearby, represents the resort and the course is a lot like him: tough, demanding on the short game and first-class. Every worker on the premises, from the starter to those cutting the grass, will smile and say hello.

There is no better service or better maintained course in South Florida.

The course is defined by water and elevated greens. The course is not far from the Atlantic Ocean, meaning the wind comes into play often.

The elevated greens come early and often. The second hole, a 536-yard par 5, has a shallow but wide green sitting up behind a lake that stretches 185 yards back down the right side of the fairway. The third hole, a 208-yard par 3, has the same shaped green, also fronted by water. Actually every par 3 has a carry over water.

And so do all the par 5s, which are the best holes on the course.

No. 6 is 539 yards and a rare straight-away hole, but there is water around the peninsula green, making it a three-shot hole.

The back side gets tougher, with water coming into play on the last six holes. No. 11 is a 503-yard par 5 with an elevated green behind a lake that guards the left side and most of the front. The green is long and narrow.

The course's signature hole is the last one, a 545-yard par 5 that tempts you to make the wrong decision on every shot. The fairway is narrow and there is a huge lake that begins 250 yards off the tee and runs down the right side of the hole. There is a large island green in that lake. The fairway curls right toward the green, which sits off to the right, parallel to the last 70 yards of the fairway.

There is little to spray a drive off the tee. There is water right (another lake) and trees left. Since the green is off to the right, the temptation is great to go for it after a good drive. If you don't, you must make sure your approach hugs the right side—and the water—to give you a good shot at birdie. Your approach must carry the water and a kidney-shaped bunker and stick on the island green, so it needs to come in high.

S C O R E C A R D

Region: Southeast

Address: 19999 W. Country Club Drive, North Miami Beach

Phone: (305) 932-6200

Access: Resort guests only.

Yardage: 7,003-5,581

Par: 36/36, 72

Green fees: $50 to $95.

What the Panelists said:

"Turnberry is a fun experience. Setting is memorable, as is the 18th hole."
—Dave Sheinin (25).

26. BAYTOWNE GOLF CLUB, SANDESTIN RESORT

Baytowne is three nines and three courses in one. All three nines are great fun and in excellent shape. There is lots of water, lots of sand and some surprising elevation changes. Sandestin, an oceanfront resort with 63 holes of golf, has spent lots of money to improve the resort and it shows on the golf courses. They are all in great shape.

Baytowne is exactly what resort golf should be like: an excellent layout that is not overbearing, but provides a good challenge.

Here's a quick tour:

The Harbor nine has water on every hole. It is the shortest of the three nines, but the one with the most trouble. No. 9 is a 529-yard par 5 that turns 90-degrees right around a cluster of bunkers. There is water on both sides of the fairway up until the dogleg.

The Troon nine features an island par 3 on the third hole (178 yards) and a tough par 4 on No. 7. The hole is long—424 yards from the back tees—and bends right toward a green protected by water on the left and in the back.

Dunes was my favorite nine. No 4 is a long (464 yards) narrow par 4 uphill to a small elevated green. The entire right side of the fairway is the side of a hill, which makes the hole look like a chute. No. 5 is a downhill par 4 (366 yards) with water on the right. No. 6 is a long, beautiful par 5 (586 yards) that bends left to an elevated green.

No. 7 is a brutish, 433-yard par 4 with a tough approach to a green bulkheaded on the left side, where a lake comes into play.

S C O R E C A R D

Region: Northwest

Address: 9300 Highway 98 West

Phone: (904) 267-8155

Access: Open to the public.

Yardage: Harbor/Troon—6,891–4,884; Troon/Dunes—7,185–5,158; Dunes/Harbor—6,890–4,862.

Par: 36/36/36.

Green fees: $55–$75.

Panelist: "Resort golf with an extraordinary attention to detail. Superior facilities, dining, and accommodations with diverse activities for all family members." —Earl Daniels (4).

27. ISLAND COURSE, INNISBROOK HILTON RESORT

One of my favorite courses at my favorite resort in Florida. This course just defines fun. It is a course you are convinced you can dominate—until it kicks you silly.

The first six holes are fairly flat, with the water mostly on the sides. The middle six holes traverse some rolling, wooded hills. The final six holes have a little bit of everything, including a great finishing hole.

The entire first hole is a peninsula, with water on both sides of the fairway and behind the green. The third hole is probably the toughest par 4 on the course. It is 445 yards long through pine trees to a green guarded by three huge bunkers.

No. 7 is the toughest par 5 (561 yards), a dogleg left that skirts a lake on the right to an elevated green protected by three large bunkers.

No. 9 is a warm-up for No. 18. A 418-yard par 4, you must bomb a drive down the tree-lined fairway to get to the corner because the hole turns straight left toward a green with water in front.

Nos. 10 and 11 will get your attention quickly on the back nine. The first is an uphill 440-yard par 4 that plays longer than it looks (as if it had to). The second is a par 5 through a forest. The fairway is narrow and the green is small, making this a three-shot hole (be smart and hit an iron off the tee to keep the ball in play).

No. 18 is a hole I could play all day, over and over again. A sharp dogleg left like No. 9, it is a little shorter and tougher. Your approach,

S C O R E C A R D

Region: Southwest
Address: U.S. highway 19 South, Tarpon Springs
Phone: (813) 942-2000.
Access: Resort guests only.
Yardage: 6,999–5,892.
Par: 36/36, 72
Green fees: $50 to $90.
Panelist: "Might be more difficult for the average player than Copperhead."
   —Bob Harig (16).

off a downhill lie, must clear two fingers of the same lake which stick out in front of the green, which slopes toward the water.

The Island Course is one of three Top 100 courses at Innisbrook—Copperhead is No. 2 and Sandpiper is No. 87.

Lots of water and narrow fairways—such as No. 18 here—define the Island Course at Copperhead.

28. LELY FLAMINGO ISLAND CLUB

With palm trees in the bunkers, and water all around the hole, the signature par 3 fifth hole is a dramatic creation by Robert Trent Jones Sr. The rest of the course is just as nice.

With bold mounds that define the fairways, lots of bunkers and rock-lined greens, Lely Flamingo is a beautiful course. The course is fairly wide open and in great shape.

Jones designed a course that is interesting to play over and over because many of the holes have more than one way to attack them.

The eighth and ninth holes are two examples. No. 8 is a 559-yard par 5 that turns left about halfway down. Carry the bunker on the left side of the fairway (276 yards from the back, 235 yards from the whites) and you have a shot at getting home in two. Or you can play it down the right side and lay up on your second shot in front of the bunker in the middle of the fairway 100 yards from the long, narrow green.

No. 9 is a par 4 (422 yards) with two fairways separated by a huge bunker. The left side is elevated and the safest way. You can gamble and go down the right side, straight toward the lake that sits in front of the green.

The choices continue on No. 13, a dogleg right par 4 that favors a fade off the tee. You can play it safe and aim for the left-center of the fairway, leaving a long second shot, or you can try and carry the bunker on the right side of the dogleg.

You don't have much choice on No. 17, a great hole where par is a great score. The dogleg left par 4 (422 yards) has trees along the left side and bunkers on the right. Your approach shot will be with a middle to long iron, over water to an elevated green with three tiers. Have fun.

S C O R E C A R D

Region: Southwest
Address: 8004 Lely Resort Blvd., Naples
Phone: (813) 793-2223
Access: Open to the public.
Yardage: 7,171–5,377.
Par: 36/36, 72
Green fees: $40–$95.
Panelist: "Great condition. Very tough. Good tournament course."
　　—Larry Gantzer (0).

29. WEST COURSE, GOLF CLUB OF MIAMI

Jackie Gleason lived here. The PGA Tour held an annual tournament here. And until recently, the PGA Tour managed the course.

Today, the course has a new clubhouse and new management. Dade County took the course back from the PGA Tour and hired a private company to operate it. The course has evolved into one of the best in South Florida.

Designed by Robert Trent Jones and updated by Bobby Weed (TPC–Tampa Bay) when the PGA Tour came in during the 1980s, the course today has among the best greens in the area. In the past few years it has hosted many of the area's biggest tournaments, including PGA and Senior PGA Tour qualifiers.

The course has water on many holes but it is almost all lateral. You need a good driver and good short game to score well here.

The sixth through ninth holes are the course's trademark. No. 6 is a brutally long par 4 (461 yards) to a long, narrow green protected by three bunkers.

No. 7 is a 556-yard par 5 that tails left to a three-tiered, elevated green surrounded by deep bunkers. The long (215 yards) par 3 No. 8 has a massive elevated green with water on the left. Whatever club you think you need on this tee, take an extra one.

No. 9 is a dogleg left par 4 (425 yards), that plays slightly downhill to a green guarded by water on the right. Long hitters can cut the corner by going over the bunker on the left side of the fairway.

The Golf Club of Miami also includes another Top 100 layout—the East Course (No. 79)—a top-flight par 62 South Course, two driving ranges, a family golf center, putting and chipping greens, and an excellent restaurant. It is the best public golf complex in Southeast Florida.

S C O R E C A R D

Region: Southeast
Address: 6801 Miami Gardens Dr., Miami
Phone: (305) 829-8456
Access: Open to the public.
Yardage: 7,017–5,298.
Par: 36/36, 72
Green fees: Under $50.
Panelist: "A subtle and difficult test that never fails to surprise, no matter how often one plays."—Joe Oglesby (15).

30. DEER CREEK GOLF CLUB (DEERFIELD BEACH)

Architect Arthur Hills came in and took a good course and made it great. Franklin Golf Properties, which bought the course in 1987, has spent $8 million upgrading the Key West-style clubhouse and renovating the golf course.

The result has been the best facility in Broward County (Ft. Lauderdale area), and one of the best in Southeast Florida.

Hills' renovation brought all the greens up to USGA specifications. He also redesigned all the tee boxes, fairway bunkers, and 14 of the 18 fairways. Another set of tees was added, increasing the course's length from 6,732 yards to 7,038 yards. The course now has more contoured fairways and more undulating greens.

Since the renovations, the course has been maintained in excellent condition. It teases you with hints of a northern course layout, with some elevation changes and rolling fairways. The tree-lined course does not feel crowded by houses, too often a problem in South Florida.

The course is also fun to play, with many good risk/reward holes. On No. 13, a 534-yard par 5, there is a lake in the middle of the fairway. Hit a good drive and you can go for it. If not, you lay up and rely on your short game.

S C O R E C A R D

Region: Southeast
Address: 2801 Country Club Blvd., Deerfield Beach
Phone: (305) 421-5550
Access: Open to the public.
Yardage: 7,038-5319.
Par: 36/36, 72
Green fees: $50 to $100.
Panelist: "Well-balanced holes; Excellent pace of play on a daily basis. Super conditions."—Marty Martinez (0).

31. RAVINES GOLF CLUB

Ravines is the hilliest course you will play in Florida. One of the state's great secrets, this course has some spectacular holes and some of the most exhilarating tee shots in the state.

Located in a suburb southeast of Jacksonville, Ravines is a resort with some homes on the grounds. Almost none are visible from the course, which winds through a forest and over, of course, several ravines.

The sight of your ball traversing the ravines or falling to a green far below your feet is a welcome change from the usual Florida course.

The fun begins on the second hole, a 360-yard par 4 that turns left after clearing a ravine on your tee shot. The carry is 214 yards from the back tees, 183 yards from the whites.

The signature hole is No. 4, a 422-yard par 4 where you need to clear two ravines, one on your tee shot and another on your approach. The green seems like an island sticking up from the ravine. It is the prettiest approach on the course.

The scenic par 4 No. 18 also has two ravines to carry, but my favorite hole is No. 9—the second-best golf hole in Florida, behind the famous island No. 17 at TPC–Stadium Course.

Every shot on this three-shot par 5 is great. You have to play this from the back tees (or at least take a look). You tee off from way up high, through a chute of trees, over a large creek to a fairway that slopes downhill and to the right. The shot seems to stay in the air forever.

The second shot is over a creek, down a fairway that starts to go uphill. Your approach is to a green up on a plateau, about 25 feet above the fairway. When someone asks me to define a memorable hole, I describe this one.

S C O R E C A R D

Region: Northeast
Address: 2932 Ravines Road, Middleburg
Phone: (904) 282-7888.
Access: Open to the public.
Yardage: 6,733–4,817
Par: 36/36, 72
Green fees: Under $50.
Panelist: "Probably the most spectacular course in Florida. Lots of elevation changes and a few trips across very deep ravines."—Fred Seely (7).

32. EMERALD BAY

The back nine at Emerald Bay is among the most scenic of any course in Northwest Florida. The course, which opened in 1993, winds through a forest and has some nice views along Choctaw Bay.

It is a precision course, where it helps to know where the trouble lies. There are times when you must lay up in front of trouble that may not be visible from the tee. You also need to be in the right spot to hit the greens, many of which have ridges and multiple tiers.

No. 10 is a long par 4 (455 yards) with water along the left side of the fairway and forest along the right. The water circles behind the green—but chances are you won't be going over this green.

No. 11 (349 yards, par 4) is a scenic hole, a thick forest lining the left side of the dogleg that wraps around it. The green is tiny and surrounded by trees. There is no room for error.

The par 3 No. 12 (229 yards) calls for a tee shot through a chute of trees and over a marsh to a large green. No. 13 is as simple as it is pretty. It's a straight-away par 5, no water, no marshes. Except it's 611 yards long and a thick forest lines both sides of the fairway.

The short par 3 No. 16 is only 166 yards from the back tees, but you're hitting onto a crowned green. The bay is off to the right of the green. You finish the round with a par 4 and a par 5, both of which require carries over water.

S C O R E C A R D

Region: Northwest

Address: 40001 Emerald Coast Parkway, Destin

Phone: (904) 837-5197

Access: Open to the public

Yardage: 6,802–5,184

Par: 36/36, 72

Green fees: $50–$90

Panelist: "An excellent Bob Cupp design. Some neat scenic routing of a couple of holes along Choctaw Bay. Always immaculately conditioned." —Ted Raymond (7).

33. SILVER COURSE, DORAL PARK

Have you seen that American Express commercial, the one with the guys putting on an island green and the bridge to the green is the American Express Card? That's No. 14 here. American Express didn't have to go far to find it either. One of its corporate offices is about a mile down the road.

The course was designed by Robert von Hagge, who worked with the late Dick Wilson on the four courses next door at the Doral Resort. Doral Park is a separate residential community and is not affiliated with the resort.

The course was private for a short time in 1994, but has returned to semi-private and is open every day to the public. It has a beautiful new clubhouse that overlooks the 18th green.

Besides the water all around the 14th green, there also is water on every other hole. The fairways are all defined by dramatic mounds, some which rise more than 20 feet high. Missing the fairway here can kill you because not only is the rough pretty thick—the mounds produce terrible stances and lies. Many of the greens are elevated and usually very fast.

The course was changed from a par 71 to 70 when the No. 3 hole was converted from an easy par 5 to a very tough par 4. It is a severe dogleg right of 465 yards with a massive bunker in the middle of the fairway short of the elevated green.

S C O R E C A R D

Region: Southeast
Address: 5001 NW 104th Ave.
Phone: (305) 594-0954
Access: Open to the public.
Yardage: 6,801–5,064
Par: 35/35, 70
Green fees: $25 to $75
Panelist: "Interesting golf course. Tricked up slightly because of all the uneven lies. Definitely a thinking man's course."—John Norton (0).

34. ROLLING OAKS, WORLD WOODS

Standing on the 150-foot high elevated tee on the par 3 eighth hole, the understated beauty of Rolling Oaks spreads out before you. The 174-yard hole requires you to carry a rock-lined creek to a two-tiered green. You have to walk across the rocks in the creek to get to the green. A low waterfall completes the picture.

Behind the green, the wide ninth fairway stretches away from you, both sides lined by oak trees. While its more celebrated sister course, Pine Barrens, slaps you with dramatic mounding and eye-catching waste areas, Rolling Oaks comes at you more quietly.

Architect Tom Fazio, who designed both courses, wanted so much to make sure that Pine Barrens and Rolling Oaks were different that he insisted on two different construction companies to build each course.

Wide-open fairways, rolling fairways and big greens that allow you to play bump-and-run create a more traditional course. There is more water on Rolling Oaks than Pine Barrens, but less sand. It is a classic course, with traditional tee boxes and subtle challenges. A large oak tree guards the left side of one of the greens, for example, so the best tee shot needs to stay right in order to give the best angle to the green.

Rolling Oaks comes across as an expansive course. The fairways, though tree-lined, are so wide the trees do not impose. The greens, though double- and triple-tiered, are so big they do not intimidate. Until you have to putt. The par 5s can be reached in two if you hit a good drive.

Everything about Rolling Oaks evokes tranquillity. There are no homes anywhere on the property. And with 800 acres on which to lay out two golf courses, crowding the holes in was not an issue.

S C O R E C A R D

Region: Central
Address: 17590 Ponce de Leon Blvd., Brooksville
Phone: (904) 796-5500
Access: Open to the public
Yardage: 6,985–5,245
Par: 36/36, 72
Green fees: $40 and up
Panelist: "Classic North Carolina-type course. Beautiful par 3s; No. 8 is most beautiful in Florida." —Rafael Miguel (21).

The signature par 3 No. 8 at World Woods' Rolling Oaks Course.

35. EMERALD HILLS

Hidden from sight in a well-established neighborhood between Miami and Ft. Lauderdale, and hidden from mind for many years because it was a private course, Emerald Hills is one of those great secrets you don't want to tell too many people about because you're scared it will ruin the fun.

Another well-designed course by Robert von Hagge and Bruce Devlin (Key Biscayne, Doral Park, Ft. Myers' Eastwood), Emerald Hills has one of the best finishing holes in Florida.

Your round here—which includes the state's most elevated green at the par No. 4—will be determined in great part by how you play three key holes: 5, 15 and 18.

No. 5 is a 548-yard par 5 that turns left. The key here is your third shot. The kidney-shaped green is bulkheaded and guarded by a lake in front and a huge mound in the back. A small pot bunker in front of the green—similar to the one on No. 17 at the TPC–Stadium Course —forces you to be even more precise.

No. 15 is a dogleg right that curves around a lake up by the green. You need to hit a good strong tee shot that fades a little to be in the best position. This two-tiered green is also bulkheaded and a back right pin placement is real tough to shoot at.

No. 18 is a par 5 that no one reaches in two. It is 592 yards long, water all along the left, out of bounds on the right and a creek in front of yet another bulkheaded green. The water curls around the right side of the long, narrow green and a bunker protects the left side. There is no room to bail out here.

· S C O R E C A R D

Region: Southeast

Address: 4100 North Hills Drive, Hollywood

Phone: (305) 961-4000

Access: Open to the public.

Yardage: 7,003–5,032

Par: 36/36, 72

Green fees: Under $75

Panelist: "Great variety of holes. Some elevated greens and memorable island greens." —Joe Oglesby (15)

---

36. BAYTREE NATIONAL

This new Gary Player-designed course in Melbourne has a little of everything: marshland, water, forest and a unique red shale waste area that sometimes runs for more than 100 yards on the side of a hole.

No. 10 is a good example: a 389-yard par 4, there is marsh down the entire right side and a 108-yard long red shale waste area down the left side and behind the green. Palm trees are spread throughout the red shale, a place where you can ground your club and drive your cart (it is not fun to hit from, though).

The next hole shows how Player got creative to make a flat piece of land and interesting golf hole. The 372-yard, par 4, No. 11 has the red shale area to the right of the fairway and a lake hidden behind some mounds on the left side. You can't see the lake from the tee, but you can drive into it. You can go at the mounds with a long iron and have a shorter approach, or play it safe down the right side.

No. 15 may be the toughest. The long (447 yards) par 4 requires a 212-yard carry over a lake off the tee. The ever-present red shale waste area runs the entire length of the hole along the left side. A dense forest beautifully frames the green, which slopes uphill.

The course is in great shape, there is a huge range and practice green and a 5,000-square foot clubhouse. It is across the street from the new Space Coast Stadium, the spring training home of the Florida Marlins.

S C O R E C A R D

Region: Central

Address: 8207 National Drive, Melbourne

Phone: (407) 259-9060

Access: Open to the public.

Yardage: 7,043–4,803

Par: 36/36, 72

Green fees: $27–$68

Panelist: "A new course, well designed and well maintained. Waste areas are a different touch."—Kevin Hayes (15).

37. METROWEST COUNTRY CLUB

This fine Robert Trent Jones Sr. layout is very popular with local golfers because it demands every shot and club in your bag. Jones, who also designed Lely Flamingo in Naples (No. 28), took advantage of the subtle elevation changes throughout the course to come up with a variety of different holes.

There are sweeping doglegs around a lake, greens with 40-foot deep hollows in front of them, fairways that slope toward the water, and a great view of the Orlando skyline from the No. 13 tee.

On the front side, No. 4 is a beautiful, long (610 yards) par 5 that turns straight right the last 120 yards. Your tee shot is between a lone oak tree and a cluster of bunkers. From there, the bunker slopes severely from left to right, so your second shot needs to stay well left of the bunker at the dogleg.

On the back side, No. 14 will play longer than the 562 yards because your second and third shots are uphill to a green surrounded by water on three sides. The only bailout area is short and right, but there are two bunkers there.

No. 18 is a solid par 4, 413 yards, with water along the left and water right and in front of the green. You need a good drive because the green is protected by bunkers left and there is no room to miss around the green.

S C O R E C A R D

Region: Central

Address: 2100 S. Hiawassee Road, Orlando

Phone: (407) 299-8800

Access: Open to the public.

Yardage: 7,051–5,325

Par: 36/36, 72

Green fees: $50–$75

Panelist: "Challenging layout with some great holes. No. 9 especially is a tough hole: dogleg left around a lake." —Paige Phillips (0).

38. FALCON'S FIRE

The third new Rees Jones courses in Florida's Top 50, Falcon's Fire has all of the signature Rees Jones trademarks: extensive mounding along the fairways to frame each hole, large greens with multiple pin locations and a fair test of golf.

Jones built Falcon's Fire before LPGA International in Daytona Beach and Sandestin's Burnt Pine, but it most resembles LPGA International. Both were built up from a mostly flat piece of land. At Falcon's Fire, the emphasis is on playability for the tourist golfer looking for a country club setting at a daily fee course.

A computer on every cart instantly gives you the yardage left to the hole and a friendly tip on how the hole plays. The course is always in great shape and the service is excellent.

The landing areas are generous and there are only a handful of forced carries over water. Two of them are beauties. No. 8 is a long par 3 (224 yards from the gold tees, 203 from the blues) with a full carry over a lake to a green surrounded by seven bunkers.

No. 13, the course's signature hole, is a long dogleg right with a daunting tee shot over water to a fairway that goes right and away from you. You do have a choice of several targets from the tee to aim for—14 pot bunkers that line the left side of the fairway (aim for the 7th bunker).

While the course is mostly water, sands and mounds, there are several tall cypress groves that frame a few holes. On No. 14, a par 5 with water all along the right side, the trees form a great backdrop behind the green.

S C O R E C A R D

Region: Central

Address: 3200 Seralago Blvd., Kissimmee

Phone: 407-932-5007

Access: Open to the public.

Yardage: 6,901–5,417

Par: 36/36, 72.

Green fees: $35 –$100.

Panelist: "This course has great potential. A necessary stop if you're going to be in Orlando. Thick rough and fair-sized greens makes it among my favorites. A lot of water." —Richard LoGello (8).

39. FOX HOLLOW GOLF CLUB

This new course northwest of Tampa is one of Florida's hidden secrets. Robert Trent Jones Sr. designed this course across this vast expanse of land that includes forests, marshes and creeks. The course's trademarks are excellent greens and those bunkers shaped like jigsaw puzzle pieces, much like Jones did at Lely Flamingo (No. 28).

The greens are huge, but they have humps, ridges and hollows to make sure you don't take any putt for granted. There are also six sets of tees, with the back black tees stretching the course to an obscene 7,138 yards.

The best holes are two cut through a forest and the intimidating No. 18. No. 3 is the toughest par 4 on the course, 451 yards and trees lining both sides of the fairway. There are only two bunkers on this hole, one on each side of the green.

The other "forest" hole is No. 11, a 558-yard par 5 that begins with a 220-yard carry from the back tees over a lake. Trees line both sides of the fairway once you clear the lake and the best approach is from the right, bunkerless side.

The finishing hole is dramatic, with the elevated fairway and a green that is one long peninsula with water on three sides. You have another 200-yard carry over water from the back tees to the start of the fairway. The green sits behind a small pot bunker on the left and has a long narrow bunker on the right. This is a good test of golf in a very peaceful setting.

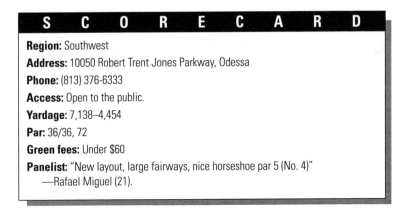

S C O R E C A R D

Region: Southwest

Address: 10050 Robert Trent Jones Parkway, Odessa

Phone: (813) 376-6333

Access: Open to the public.

Yardage: 7,138–4,454

Par: 36/36, 72

Green fees: Under $60

Panelist: "New layout, large fairways, nice horseshoe par 5 (No. 4)"
— Rafael Miguel (21).

40. GATEWAY GOLF CLUB

Designed by the same architect, Tom Fazio, and developed by the same company, Westinghouse Communities, as Pelican's Nest (No. 11), Gateway is naturally compared to its sister course to the south.

So let's compare. The service is the same (excellent), down to the ice-filled coolers on every cart. The courses are much different. At Gateway, there is more room off the fairways and the mounding throughout the course is more dramatic.

There is also much more sand. Fazio incorporated Cape Cod bunkers and extensive use of stands of native cypress head to give the course more of a northern feel than the mangrove-lined Pelican's Nest.

The front side is a links-style with few tees, but lots of sand. On No. 3, a 408-yard par 4, four pot bunkers guard the left side of the green and a long narrow bunker stretches for more than 100 yards down the right side of the fairway, all the way to the front of the green.

The back nine has more trees, especially around the 10th, 12th and 14th greens, where cypresshead serve as the backdrop on each hole.

No. 18 is a good finishing hole, a double dogleg with water all along the left side and a collection of five bunkers around the green.

S C O R E C A R D

Region: Southwest
Address: 11360 Championship Dr., Ft. Myers
Phone: (813) 561-1010
Access: Open to the public.
Yardage: 6,974–5,323
Par: 36/36, 72
Green fees: $30–$90.
Panelist: "Gateway's extensive mounding and numerous bunkers make your round very challenging. The par 3s are tough and the par 5s are as long as any course in Southwest Florida." —Bill Janney (18).

41. WINDSOR PARKE GOLF CLUB

The Jacksonville area has some of the best daily fee courses in Florida. There are three that stand out—Windsor Parke, Queen's Harbour (No. 45) and Cimarrone (No. 46). They all have great service and excellent course conditions on three very different courses.

At Windsor Parke, tall pines provide scenic backdrops on many holes and water lines half of the fairways. The Arthur Hills design provides a strong test and makes good use of long and short holes.

Holes 6 through 9 all have water lining the entire side of the fairway—the left side on 7, 8 and 9—with the water creeping in front of the green on Nos. 6 and 9. The holes aren't terribly long and using a 3-wood off the tee is wise on Nos. 6 and 9 to keep the ball in play.

No. 13 is tough par 4 (409 yards) with water left the entire length of the hole. The green sits low by the water. No. 15 is a 556-yard par five with a creek running in front of the green, making this a three-shot hole.

The prettiest hole is No. 16, a 194-yard par 3 over water to a low-lying green with a long, narrow bunker circling around half of the green.

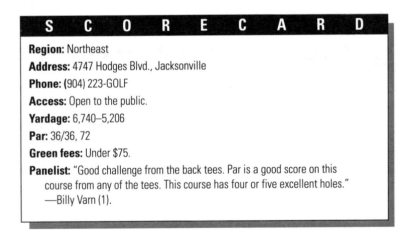

SCORECARD

Region: Northeast

Address: 4747 Hodges Blvd., Jacksonville

Phone: (904) 223-GOLF

Access: Open to the public.

Yardage: 6,740–5,206

Par: 36/36, 72

Green fees: Under $75.

Panelist: "Good challenge from the back tees. Par is a good score on this course from any of the tees. This course has four or five excellent holes." —Billy Varn (1).

42. HIDDEN CREEK

Hidden Creek, a Ron Garl design, is one of the more enjoyable courses in the Panhandle. Ron Garl, who designed many courses in Southwest Florida, came north with his trademark long bunkers.

There is plenty of sand, but very little water. There is only one forced carry on the entire course—the 200-yard par 3 over water. The greens are large and the fairways, many lined with tall pines, are generous.

The most dramatic holes are on the back nine, where there is no water at all. No. 11 is stunning, a 382-yard par 4 that turns left to a green that has a bulkhead in front, elevating it up from the massive bunker in front of the green. Wooden steps on the left side get you up to the green.

No. 12 is par 5 (537 yards) that calls for a tee shot over a large bunker to a terraced fairway that sits higher than the surrounding rough on the left. Three small pot bunkers protect the front of the green. On No. 15 (par 5, 556 yards), your tee shot must clear a huge grass swale before the fairway begins. A large bunker short and right of the green makes you think twice about blasting away at the green.

The course has hosted U.S. Open qualifying tournaments and has excellent service.

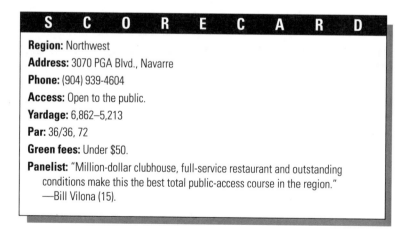

S C O R E C A R D

Region: Northwest

Address: 3070 PGA Blvd., Navarre

Phone: (904) 939-4604

Access: Open to the public.

Yardage: 6,862–5,213

Par: 36/36, 72

Green fees: Under $50.

Panelist: "Million-dollar clubhouse, full-service restaurant and outstanding conditions make this the best total public-access course in the region." —Bill Vilona (15).

43. QUEEN'S HARBOUR

Another of the many fine daily fee golf courses in the Jacksonville area, Queen's Harbour features a beautiful back nine and water almost every hole. There is water cutting across the fairway, surrounding greens and running down both sides of the fairway. There is even an island tee box, on No. 10.

The course is popular with locals and is always in good shape. A taste on the prevalence of water: On No. 4, a 416-yard par 4, you must hit over water on your tee shot and on your approach shot. The green has water in front and behind the green.

But the course gets its high marks for its back nine, beautiful holes meandering through the flats next to the Intracoastal, which serves as the water hazard on No. 18. After your tee shot off the island tee on No. 10, your approach is to a green guarded by water to the right. No. 12 is a double dogleg par 5 (522 yards) with water guarding the green on the left side. No. 13 is a par 3 (174 yards) with carry all over, you guessed it, water.

No. 17 is a par 5 (549 yards) dogleg left with a fairway split by a lake. Your second and third shots must carry water.

Despite the abundance of water, Queen's Harbour is not an overly difficult test. The course is very playable and panelists constantly commented on its fairness and high reward factor for good shots. The greens are excellent and not too difficult.

S C O R E C A R D

Region: Northeast

Address: 13361 Atlantic Blvd., Jacksonville

Phone: 904-221-1012

Access: Open to the public.

Yardage: 7,012–5,139

Par: 36/36, 72

Green fees: $30 to $60.

Panelist: "It borders the St. John's River and Intracoastal Waterway and has 18 solid holes. It's a good course for everyone. Very playable from the middle tees, tough from the back." —Fred Seely (7).

44. CIMARRONE GOLF & COUNTRY CLUB

They work on their greens at night, so as not to disturb play. That is commitment. The greens are Cimarrone are among the best in the region. Many are undulating and all are fairly fast. They are a joy to putt.

The course is set amid 17 interwoven lakes that bring water or marshland into play on every hole.

Cimarrone gets your attention right away. The first hole is a dogleg right, 530-yard par 5. Your tee shot is over marshland and your approach must carry close to 200 yards.

It doesn't let up until the last hole, a 439-yard par 4 with water a factor on both the tee shot and the approach.

My favorite hole on the course was No. 10, a dogleg right par 4. Your tee shot is straight out toward a forest at the end of the fairway. A wide creek cuts in front of the secluded green surrounded by mounds and tucked into a stand of tall pines.

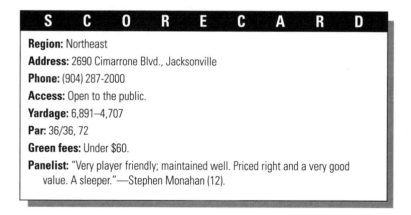

S C O R E C A R D

Region: Northeast

Address: 2690 Cimarrone Blvd., Jacksonville

Phone: (904) 287-2000

Access: Open to the public.

Yardage: 6,891–4,707

Par: 36/36, 72

Green fees: Under $60.

Panelist: "Very player friendly; maintained well. Priced right and a very good value. A sleeper."—Stephen Monahan (12).

45. DIAMONDBACK GOLF CLUB

This is my pick for the next great course in Florida. Everything about this new course—it opened in early 1995—was done right. A group of members at Grenelefe decided they wanted their own club and purchased the land across the street.

They hired Joe Lee, who did the original three courses at Walt Disney World, and gave him free reign. The result is breath-taking. Winding through a wooded setting with rolling terrain, the course looks like it has been there for years. There are no houses anywhere on the course and almost all of the fairways are lined on at least one side by woods.

The highlights are Nos. 16 and 18, two dramatic holes that play off each other. No. 16 is a dogleg left par 5 (524 yards) that sits atop a plateau, overlooking No. 18 below. The 16th fairway wraps around a lake that has a waterfall cascading down to the 18th fairway. After it turns, the 16th fairway descends to a green guarded by four bunkers.

No. 18 is a great finishing hole, a 441-yard dogleg right par 4. You aim your tee shot at the waterfall on the left and you have a slightly uphill approach to a green guarded on the left by water.

Since it's so new and tucked out of the way, the course is not well known and not very crowded. Once word gets out, that will change.

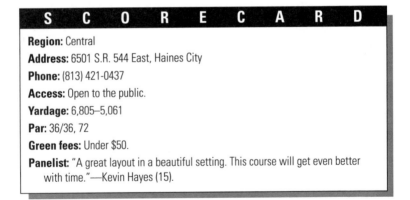

S C O R E C A R D

Region: Central

Address: 6501 S.R. 544 East, Haines City

Phone: (813) 421-0437

Access: Open to the public.

Yardage: 6,805–5,061

Par: 36/36, 72

Green fees: Under $50.

Panelist: "A great layout in a beautiful setting. This course will get even better with time."—Kevin Hayes (15).

46. BLUEWATER BAY RESORT

The first tee on the Lake nine juts out into a lake. Your tee shot carries the lake and disappears over a hill that makes it appear there is nowhere for your shot to land. So begins the round at Bluewater Bay, a 36-hole complex in the aptly named town of Niceville.

Fazio designed the first 18 holes, the Lake, Marsh and Bay nines, and Jerry Pate designed the Magnolia course. All are excellent nines. The original 18 holes have a certain charm that captivate you. They can also suffocate you if you don't hit the ball straight. Many of the holes wind through pine trees, making accuracy extremely important.

No. 3 on the Lake course is a fabulous par 4, a 420-yard hole with a canal running down the left side of the fairway. The fairway is elevated and your approach shot is over the canal and down to a severely sloping green.

On the Bay course, the highlight is No. 6, a 370-yard par 4 that demands an approach over marshland to a green that sits in front of Choctawhatchee Bay. The view is stunning.

If you want bay views, play the Marsh course, where holes 4, 5 and 8 run along the bay. No. 4 is a par 4 to an island green surrounded by marshland.

Magnolia is the newest course and has the most room around the fairways. Holes 4, 5 and 6 play through marshland. The tees on No. 6 are islands in the middle of the marshland.

S C O R E C A R D

Region: Northwest

Address: 1950 Bluewater Blvd., Niceville

Phone: (904) 897-3241

Access: Open to the public.

Yardage: Bay—3,318–2,630; Lake—3,485–2,748; Marsh—3,362–2,544; Magnolia—3,307–2,499.

Par: 36/36/36/36

Green fees: Under $50.

Panelist: "Well-manicured course with excellent clubhouse facilities. Four nines provide variety. Shot-makers course for straight hitters." —Earl Daniel (4).

47. TPC–VALLEY COURSE

Pete Dye designed a more conventional—and easier—course to complement the Stadium Course (No. 1). Sure, there is water on every single hole, but there is also room. You can run the ball onto the greens and most of the water is lateral. The course, home to the Senior Players Championship, is as well-maintained as the Stadium Course.

Don't get lulled into thinking this is an easy course. Many of the greens are protected on one side by water, which makes approach shots tough. On. No. 2, a 227-yard par 3, your shot must carry water all the way to the green.

The par 5s are all very good. No. 7 (559 yards) sweeps left, water along the left. The green sticks out into the lake, which makes it difficult to try and go for it in two.

There are also three long par 4s to test your driving ability. No. 9 (429 yards) is a dogleg left with a canal all along the left side and a huge bunker guarding the left side of the green. No. 15 is longer—462 yards—and tougher because the hole sweeps right to a green protected on the right by water.

The finishing hole, 436 yards, is guarded by trees on the left and water on the right. The bulkheaded green has water to the right and bunkers in the back.

S C O R E C A R D

Region: Northeast

Address: 1000 TPC Blvd., Ponte Vedra Beach

Phone: (904) 285-7777

Access: Resort guests only.

Yardage: 6,864-5,126

Par: 36/36, 72

Green fees: $100 and up.

Panelist: "Gets less play than the famed Stadium Course, so is usually in great shape. An interesting design with a good mixture of holes. Numerous mounding and hills create unique shots for Florida." —Barry Turnball (7).

48. TIMACUAN GOLF & COUNTRY CLUB

Of all the Ron Garl designs in Florida, and there a lot of them, this is the most un-Garl-like course. This is really two different courses in one. The front nine is Scottish-links style, with wide open fairways and significant elevation changes. The back nine has more of a Carolina feel, with pine trees lining the fairways and plenty of sand.

No. 5 is a 512-yard par 5 that plays uphill. The fairway is split in two by a huge bunker that begins 200 yards from the green and stretches for 75 yards. This wouldn't be a Garl course without those huge bunkers. At the par 3 No. 7, the green is surrounded by one huge bunker that begins in front of the green and splits at the green into two branches that circle the green.

The back nine has much more water, including forced carries on the last three holes. No. 16 is a 202-yard par 3 to a virtual island green. No. 17 is a 429-yard par 4, dogleg right where you tee shot is over a lake and the green is protected by the same lake on the right.

The finishing hole is a dogleg left, (par 4, 443 yards) where the fairway and the green are separated by a huge bunker and water guards the back of the green.

S C O R E C A R D

Region: Central

Address: 550 Timacuan Blvd., Lake Mary

Phone: (407) 321-0010

Access: Open to the public.

Yardage: 7,019–5,401

Par: 36/36, 72

Green fees: Under $60.

Panelist: "A pretty well designed course that presents a good challenge to golfers of all skill levels." —Steve Riviere (2).

49. THE MOORS

Tired of the water and trees? Go to The Moors, which is different from any course in the Panhandle. There are only three lakes on the course, which brings water into play on five holes.

The Moors is a Scottish-style links course, with plenty of room around the fairways and pot bunkers around the greens. This is a new course and in November 1995 is scheduled to host the Senior PGA Tour's Emerald Coast Classic for the first time.

There are some Florida touches: Wetlands come into play on a few holes, most notably on Nos. 9 and 13. No. 9 is along and tough par 4, 455 yards, with wetlands in front of the green. The last 100 yards of your approach shot must carry the wetlands. On No. 13, the wetlands run up the ride side of the hole.

But mostly this is a wide-open layout—you can see a half-dozen holes from the pro shop—that really is a links course. No. 3 is patterned after the "Postage Stamp Hole" at Troon. The par 3 has an elevated green with a steep bunker in front. No. 4 is patterned after the famous "Road Hole" at St. Andrews.

S C O R E C A R D

Region: Northwest

Address: 3220 Avalon Blvd., Milton

Phone: (904) 995-GOLF

Access: Open to the public.

Yardage: 6,912–5,340.

Par: 36/35, 71

Green fees: Under $65.

Panelist: "Scottish-style course, complete with clubhouse designed after Muirfield." —Bill Vilona (15).

50. BILTMORE GOLF CLUB

The oldest course in the Top 50, Biltmore Golf Club opened in 1926 and hosted the Biltmore Open in the 1930s. Designed by Donald Ross, the course was renovated in 1992 and now is in excellent shape. The historic and elegant Biltmore Hotel towers in the background. Set in one of Miami's most affluent suburbs, wonderful million-dollar homes line the fairways.

The course is fairly wide-open, but the course does require you to work the ball and use every club in the bag. No. 6 is the toughest, a 391-yard par 4, that demands a good drive so you can go for the bulkheaded green, which has a canal in front.

No. 9, a dogleg left par 4 (Arnold Palmer once drove the green during a tournament) and No. 11, a dogleg left par 5, are not too tough if you can draw the ball off the tee. You will also need that draw on No. 12, a par 4 that turns left around tall trees. If you hit it straight off the tee, you will hit it through the fairway and huge oak tree on the right side of the fairway makes it almost impossible to get on the green from there.

No. 17 is a double dogleg par 5 with a canal in front of a green that slopes severely from back to front. If you cut the left corner on the tee shot, you might have a shot at the green in two, but the canal, which has a second fork also in front of the green, is about 50 yards wide in front of what is a small green.

S C O R E C A R D

Region: Southeast
Address: 1210 Anastasia Ave., Coral Gables
Phone: (305) 460-5366
Access: Open to the public
Yardage: 6,652–55,697.
Par: 35/37, 71
Green fees: Under $40.
Panelist: "Beautiful setting; usually in nice shape and a lot of fun to play."
 —Ernie Rodriguez (15).

The historic Biltmore Hotel serves as the backdrop to this municipal Donald Ross course. The PGA Tour's Miami Open used to be held here in the 1960s.

51. MARCUS POINTE NORTHWEST REGION

2500 Oak Pointe Drive, Pensacola
904-484-9770; Par: 72; Yards: 6,737–5,252.
Access: Open to the public; Green fees: Under $40.

Just 10 minutes north of Pensacola, Marcus Pointe is one of the best bargains in Northwest Florida. Situated amid 600 acres of rolling woodland, architect Earl Stone designed a course that complements the surroundings well. The fairways are lined with old pine and oak trees, and water only comes into play on No. 15.

That hole is a great par 5 (550 yards from the back) that turns right around a bunker that is 230 yards out. As it turns, the fairway turns downhill and slants toward a pond on the right corner where the fairway meets the elevated green. Marcus Pointe, which hosted the 1991 and 1992 Ben Hogan Pensacola Open, also has some of the best greens in the region.

52. EL CAMPEON, MISSION INN CENTRAL REGION

10400 County Road 48, Howey-in-the-Hills
904-324-3101; Par: 72; Yards: 6,842–5,038.
Access: Open to the public, discount for resort guests.
Green fees: $50 to $100.

Among the oldest courses in Florida, the course was built in 1926 by Scotsman C.C. Clarke and redesigned by Lloyd Clifton in 1970. With as much as 85 feet in elevation changes—phenomenal by Florida standards—the course has a unique feel.

The best hole is No. 4, a double dogleg par 5. You tee off from an elevated tee, over a stream to a narrow, tree-lined fairway. Your second shot must get you in position on the double dogleg for your third shot over a lake to an undulating green. The newer Las Colinas Course at the resort is much flatter, more wide open and lacks the character of El Campeon.

53. EAGLE PINES, WALT DISNEY WORLD CENTRAL REGION

1 Vista Dr., Lake Buena Vista
904-824-2270; Par: 72; Yards: 6,772–4,838.
Access: Open to the public, discount for resort guests.
Green fees: $50 to $100.

Pete Dye's contribution to the five-course collection at Disney World, Eagle Pines was used as one of the three courses in the PGA

The Top 100 Courses: 51 to 100   119

Tour's Oldsmobile Classic because the Lake Buena Vista Course was being renovated.

Shorter than all the other Disney courses, Eagle Pines becomes a test by bringing water into play on 16 holes. There are also massive bunkers, such as the one in front of the 14th green. The course is flatter and less dramatic visually than its neighbor Osprey Ridge (No. 19 in the Florida Top 50). But because Disney keeps all its courses in spectacular shape, the course is worth playing.

54. MATANZAS WOODS GOLF CLUB   NORTHEAST REGION

398 Lakeview Blvd., Palm Coast
904-446-6330; Par: 72; Yards: 6,985–5,348.
Access: Open to the public; Green fees: $39–52.

The best of the four courses at the Sheraton Palm Coast development, this Arnold Palmer–Ed Seay design cuts through a forest of tall pines. Matanzas Woods features rolling fairways and huge greens. The par 5s are excellent, especially Nos. 4 and 18.

Both par 5s require carry over water to get on the green; No. 4 has a lake in front and No. 18 has an island green that is huge, with three traps and pine trees in the back. Cypress Knoll, a Gary Player design which opened in 1990, has much smaller greens and more narrow fairways. It is the second-best course in the complex.

55. WESTCHASE   SOUTHWEST REGION

10307 Radcliffe Dr., Tampa
813-854-2331; Par: 72; Yards: 6,710–5,205.
Access: Open to the public; Green fees: $25–45.

The Tampa area's entry into upscale daily-fee golf is an excellent Lloyd Clifton company design that winds by a nature preserve and through a forest. Part of a planned development, the area surrounding the course is mostly undeveloped, giving the course a wonderfully secluded setting. Water and/or wetlands come into play on 16 of the 18 holes. To offset the high demand for target accuracy, the greens are not severely sloped.

The course is not exceedingly long and the long par 4s have very wide fairways. The par 3s are all good, especially Nos. 3 and 15. The third is probably the prettiest hole on the course, with bulkheaded tee box rising out of the wetlands and a green fronted by water and framed by bunkers. No. 15 is a short par 3 (160 yards from the back) with wetlands in front and to the left of the green.

56. SADDLEBROOK COURSE, SADDLEBROOK RESORT

SOUTHWEST REGION

5700 Saddlebrook Way, Wesley Chapel
813-973-1111; Par: 70; Yards: 6,603–5,183.
Access: Open to the public, discount for resort guests.
Green fees: $30–$115.

The better of the two courses at the resort, this course was the first one built here, in 1979, by Arnold Palmer. There is water on almost every hole, which gives the shortish course its bite. The undulating greens remind you a little of Palmer's Bay Hill course. Many do not have bunkers guarding the front, allowing you to run the ball onto the green.

The resort, with condos clustered in groups throughout the property, is superb—as is the huge pool adjacent to the pro shops. The courses are well maintained and very popular in the winter with out-of-state guests. In the summer, prices are cut more than in half and tee times are much easier to get.

57. THE CHAMPIONS CLUB AT SUMMERFIELD

SOUTHEAST REGION

3400 S.E. Summerfield Way, Stuart
407-283-1500. Par: 72. Yards: 6,809–5,614.
Access: Open to the public; Green fees: Under $75.

Opened in February 1994, this Tom Fazio design wanders through wetlands. No. 2 is a par 3 (197 yards from the back) over the wetlands. No. 9 is a good par 4, a dogleg left that requires you to carry wetlands on your approach. A scenic course with a good amount of wildlife, it is one of the more wide-open Fazio courses.

Having said that, wetlands do come into play on 12 of the holes. The course will not overpower you, but it does require you to hit draws and fades—and to be accurate. One of the better courses between Palm Beach and Orlando.

58. LINKS COURSE, SANDESTIN RESORT

NORTHWEST REGION

5500 Emerald Coast Parkway East, Destin
904-267-8144. Par: 72. Yards: 6,710–4,969.
Access: Open to the public; discount to resort guests.
Green fees: $55–$75.

With five holes along Choctawhatchee Bay, the course has some of the prettiest views in the area. If you hit it long on the par 4 No. 5, your ball is in the bay. Same result if you pull your approach on No. 18, a par 5 along the bay.

The course is always in good shape and requires accuracy: water or wetlands come into play on 12 holes. But the course is not over-bearing—the fairways and landing areas are generous and most of the trouble is lateral. Sandestin is a rare resort, with three excellent courses and a phenomenal beach all on the same property.

59. EASTWOOD GOLF COURSE   CENTRAL REGION

13950 Golfway Blvd., Orlando
407-281-4653; Par: 72; Yards: 7,176–5,393.
Access: Open to the public. Green fees: Under $50.

This is a course that local players love because the greens are al-ways in great shape. A shot-maker's course, water comes into play on 16 holes. No. 14 is a par with a virtual island green, but there is plenty of room for error.

The best hole is No. 10, a long par 5 (628 yards!) that turns 90 degree to the left at 225 yards. You have the option of a blind drive over the trees on the left or playing it safe down the right side. The fairway is narrow and lined with trees, the green surrounded by three bunkers.

60. UNIVERSITY PARK
COUNTRY CLUB   SOUTHWEST REGION

7671 University Park Blvd., Sarasota
813-359-9999; Par: 72; Yards: 6,951–4,914.
Access: Open to the public; Green fees: $40–$85.

One of the best maintained courses in Southwest Florida, this Ron Garl design is a no-nonsense good golf test. Garl's signature massive, snaking bunkers are here, but mostly around the tee boxes as deco-rations. The greens that have water in the front are bulkheaded and the par 3s are all excellent. Three of the four have water in front of the green, especially No. 16, aptly called "The Drink."

The course is always in great shape, the greens are excellent and the staff is among the nicest in the area.

61. BREAKERS WEST

1550 Flagler Parkway, West Palm Beach
407-790-7000. Par: 71. Yards: 6,901–5,385.
Access: Breakers resort guests only.

A hidden gem in Palm Beach County, the entire back nine has been renovated and new management has improved the course's condition to excellent. The course winds past some beautiful homes, including those of baseball star Andres Galarraga and former University of Miami quarterback Steve Walsh.

No. 9 is the signature hole, a par 4 (435 yards from the back) that turns left after clearing a lake. The tee shot has to be far enough out there to be able to clear the stand of trees left of the elevated green.

62. NAPLES BEACH
HOTEL & GOLF CLUB

851 Gulf Shore Blvd. North, Naples
813-261-2222; Par: 72; Yards: 6,497–5,267.
Access: Open to the public, discount to hotel guests.
Green fees: Under $75.

Built in the 1920s and redesigned by Ron Garl in 1979, Naples Beach has been steadily improving the course during the past few years. New sand and better fairway conditions have helped increase the popularity of what always has been a well-designed course. Garl replaced the pedestrian par 3 third hole with a completely new hole to the left of the old one. The hole now requires a middle-iron shot over a small lake to a huge elevated green.

There are other excellent holes: No. 7 is a virtual island green par 3, with the green bulkheaded. And No. 18, a dogleg right par 4 with water on both sides of the fairway is a great finishing hole.

63. HUNTER'S CREEK

14401 Sports Club Way, Orlando
407-240-4653; Par: 72; Yards: 7,432–5,755.
Access: Open to the public. Green fees: Under $50 to $100.

One of the longest courses in Florida, the course can be real hard the first time you play it. Besides needing to be long, you need to be accurate because there is water everywhere. Low handicappers love this place.

64. POLO TRACE

13397 Hagen Ranch Road, Delray Beach
407-495-5301. Par: 72; Yards: 7,096–5,314.
Access: Open to the public; Green fees: $50–$100.

The closest to Scotland you can get while still in South Florida. The work of Karl Litten and PGA pro Joey Sindelar, Polo Trace was created to resemble a links course. The course is wide open, but beware of the rough. There are also no houses lining the fairways, giving this urban course a serene setting.

The layout is interesting, with back-to-back-to-back par 5 in holes 9, 10 and 11. The entire back nine is long and tough. No. 15 is a 226-yard par 3 to an elevated green and No. 18 is a mammoth par 4—443 yards. Your approach shot must carry a bunker and a rock wall.

65. INDIGO LAKES

2620 W. International Speedway, Daytona Beach
904-254-3607; Par: 72; Yards: 7,168–5,159.
Access: Open to the public. Green fees: Under $50.

The former site of the LPGA Sprint Championships (the tournament moved to its permanent home at LPGA International, No. 22 on Florida's Top 50, in 1995), Indigo Lakes has undergone several transformations in the last few years. It has changed from a Hilton resort to a Holiday Inn resort to a public course.

The course was updated several years ago and it has helped. The greens are large and the course, with lots of woods and water, is very playable. There are four lakes that come into play on eight holes and almost 100 bunkers on the course.

66. GOLF CLUB OF MARCO

400 S. Collier Boulevard, Marco Island
813-793-6060; Par: 72; Yards: 6,898–5,416
Access: Open to the public; Green fees: $35–$90.

It's a resort course, it's near the beach and it's in Florida. You got it, there is lots of water. Like on 15 holes. To his credit, architect Joe Lee sculpted a very playable course out of all the water. The fairways are generous and the greens, though often fronted by water, are large and manageable.

The signature hole, the par 3 16th, is a full carry over a lagoon to an elevated, bulkheaded green. On No. 18 (par 4, 398 yards), your tee shot must carry water to a fairway that has water all along the right side. Your approach, if you hit it to the right side of the fairway, must also carry water.

67. HALIFAX PLANTATION NORTHEAST REGION

4000 Old Dixie Hwy., Ormond Beach
904-676-9600; Par: 72; Yards: 7,128–4,971.
Access: Open to the public; Green fees: Under $40.

This course got huge points for setting and ambiance. Even the drive from I-95 to the course, down a tree-covered highway, is pretty. The course is cut through a forest, where huge pines line both sides of the fairway. Part of an extensive residential development, there are no houses along the course, giving it an isolated setting.

Because of the forest on both sides of almost every fairway, you must keep the ball in play to score well. Bunkers in the fairways and short of some greens can play tricks on your depth perception if you are used to playing flat courses defined by water.

68. CYPRESS COURSE, PALM BEACH
POLO & COUNTRY CLUB SOUTHEAST REGION

11809 Polo Club Rd., West Palm Beach
407-798-7401. Par: 72 Yards: 7,116–5,172.
Access: Resort guests only after noon every day.
Green fees: $50–$100.

One of the best kept secrets in Palm Beach area, the P.B. and Pete Dye course is the better of the two courses at the resort. Built in 1988, this is a monster course designed for the long hitter.

Six of the par 4s measure more than 420 yards from the back tees—and four of them are more than 400 yards long from the blue tees. And then there is the 641-yard par 5 No. 17. The course is set in an exclusive setting, catering to members from the Northeast and guests of its resort.

69. BINKS FOREST COUNTRY CLUB SOUTHEAST REGION

400 Binks Drive, Wellington
407-795-0028. Par: 72; Yards: 7,091–5,468.
Access: Open to the public; Green fees: $50–$100.

Designed by PGA pro Johnny Miller, Binks Forest's holes wind through a stately pine forest, one of the few South Florida courses in a heavily wooded environment. Formerly a private club, Binks Forest was purchased by American Golf Corp. in 1994. The company operates several South Florida courses, but this is their best property.

Determined to provide a country club atmosphere for the daily fee golfer, American Golf spent about $200,000 refurbishing the course in late 1994 and early 1995. The course is an excellent test and the greens are in great shape. The course was the site of the 1990 Sazale Team Championship, won by Fred Couples and Mike Donald.

70. SOUTHERN DUNES
GOLF & COUNTRY CLUB   CENTRAL REGION

2888 Southern Dunes Blvd., Haines City
813-421-4653; Par: 72; Yards: 7,219–5,225.
Access: Open to the public. Green fees: Under $45.

Up and coming architect Steve Smyers, who lives in nearby Lakeland, designed this sand-laden gem few people outside of Central Florida have heard of. There is water on only two holes, but the sand provides plenty of challenge on this hilly course that feels more Scottish than Florida-ish. The greens are large and not too tough to read.

The two toughest holes are Nos. 13 and 18—both uphill par 4s, both longer than 460 yards from the back tees and both into the prevailing wind.

71-72. MAGNOLIA AND PALM COURSES,
WALT DISNEY WORLD   CENTRAL REGION

1 Magnolia Palm Dr., Lake Buena Vista
407-824-2270
Magnolia—Par: 72; Yards: 6,957–5,398.
Palm—Par: 72; Yards: 7,190–5,414
Access: Open to the public, discount for resort guests.
Green fees: $50–$100.

Two of the original three Disney courses, there is much debate among golfers as to which is better. Magnolia has been the final round course of the PGA Tour's Oldsmobile Classic, but the Palm Course is longer and tougher to score on.

Magnolia is more wide open, but includes 100 bunkers and 10 lakes. Palm has tree-lined fairways and more narrow fairways. Both are in superb condition.

73. OLDE HICKORY GOLF
& COUNTRY CLUB   SOUTHWEST REGION

14670 Olde Hickory Blvd., Ft. Myers
813-768-3335; Par: 72; Yards: 6,601–5,005.
Access: Open to the public; Green fees: Under $50.

Another of the Ron Garl designs that permeate Southwest Florida, this one winds through a nice residential development and is across the street from one of the region's best private courses, Fiddlesticks.

This course is short, tight and with lots of water. There are elevated greens and an island green (No. 17). There are five short par 4s—Nos. 2, 9, 10, 13 and 14—and all but No. 9 have water around the green.

74. EAST COURSE, TIGER POINT
GOLF AND COUNTRY CLUB   NORTHWEST REGION

1255 Country Club Rd., Gulf Breeze
904-932-1333. Par: 72. Yards: 7,033–5,209.
Access: Open to the public. Green fees: Under $50.

Jerry Pate designed and operated this course 10 minutes east of Pensacola. Pate threw a little bit of everything into this course: he left a tall tree in the front of the second green, a par 3 that requires you to carry water, a trap and the tree when the pin is far left. There is an island green at No. 5, a 390-yard par 4. And on No. 13, a par 5 with water in front of the green, there is a bunker—called the tiger's eye—in the middle of the green.

The best hole is No. 8, a double dogleg par 5 with a great risk-reward tee shot. You must carry a lake and a row of bunkers to a fairway that is almost perpendicular to you. Cut off enough and clear the bunkers and you can reach it in two. Or you can play safe by staying left.

75. COLONY WEST   SOUTHEAST REGION

6800 NW 88th Ave., Tamarac
305-726-8430. Par: 72; Yards: 7,271–5,422.
Access: Open to the public; Green fees: Under $50.

One of the longest courses in the region, Colony West starts with a 621-yard par 5. Designed by Bruce Devlin and Robert Von Hagge (Key Biscayne, Doral Park Silver), the course places an emphasis on length—four of the par 4s are longer than 400 yards from the white tees.

No. 12, the signature hole is a massive par 4 (452 yards from the back) with water in front of the green. The good news is there is plenty of room for you to bang away.

76. HARBOR HILLS   CENTRAL REGION

6538 Lake Griffin Road, Lady Lake
904-753-7711; Par: 72; Yards: 6,878-5,355.
Access: Open to the public. Green fees: $25 to $45.

Another of the fine courses in the middle of nowhere, Harbor Hills is a wide-open undulating course along Lake Griffin. Opened in 1989, the back nine starts with a tee shot down a hill over a road to a green framed by the lake. No. 12 is a par 5 that runs along the edge of the lake.

Once away from the lake, the course begins to get hilly. No. 17 is a par 4 where your tee shot is down one side of a hill and your approach is up the other side of the hill to the green on top of the hill. The course is in great shape and has a genuine country club feel because most of the people who play there are members.

77. DUNES COURSE, PALM BEACH
POLO & COUNTRY CLUB   SOUTHEAST REGION

11809 Polo Club Rd., West Palm Beach
407-798-7401. Par: 72 Yards: 7,050-5,516.
Access: Resort guests only; Green fees: $50 to $100.

Designed by Ron Garl and Jerry Pate, the Dunes Course is a little shorter and plays easier than its sister Cypress Course. There is plenty of water, though, to keep your attention on accuracy. Water comes into play on 16 of the 18 holes (only No. 9 and 17 are dry).

The course features the trademark Garl sand bunkers—long, snaky traps that seem to run forever. But there are also pot bunkers, extensive mounding and rolling fairways that give the course a more Scottish feel.

78. OAKWOOD GOLF CLUB   CENTRAL REGION

1000 Capps Road, Lake Wales
813-676-8558; Par: 72; Yards: 6,891–5,216.
Access: Open to the public. Green fees: Under $35.

A personal favorite, this is a true hidden gem. Winding through tree-lined fairways and wetlands, this Karl Litten design is very pretty and very playable.

The first two holes set the tone: No. 1 is a 425-yard par 4 that slopes slightly downhill and to the left. toward an elevated green. No. 2 is a par 5 that doglegs right at the end, hiding the green from view until your third shot. Wetlands at the left corner force you to be very careful with the location of your second shot. Impeccably maintained, rarely crowded and usually under $30, this place is a great deal.

79. EAST COURSE,
GOLF CLUB OF MIAMI   SOUTHEAST REGION

6801 Miami Gardens Dr., Country Club of Miami

305-829-4700—Public; Par: 70; Yards: 6,353–5,025.

Access: Open to the public; Green fees: Under $50.

Shorter than its sister West Course, the East is in the same excellent condition and is a good test from the back tees. The course places a premium on your short game and rewards accuracy over distance. The course is always in excellent condition and has one of the best clubhouses in South Florida. The course was refurbished by the PGA Tour in the 1980s, but the county took over the course in 1994.

No. 4, a par 3 that can stretch to 203 yards from the back tees, requires an approach over water to a huge two-tiered green that slopes severely to the left. No. 17 is a short par 4 over water; you can drive the green, but miss it short and/or left and you are wet.

80. GOLF CLUB OF JACKSONVILLE   NORTHEAST REGION

10440 Tournament Lane, Jacksonville
904-779-0800; Par: 71; Yards: 6,620–5,021.

Access: Open to the public; Green fees: Under $50.

Another of the PGA Tour efforts into public golf, the Tour still manages this facility (the Tour dropped out of its Golf Club of Miami project in late 1994). Designed by Bobby Weed, who recently left the PGA Tour to go out on his own, and Tour player Mark McCumber, the Golf Club enjoys the great maintenance common to all Tour properties.

The course itself features rolling fairways, lakes and tree-lined fairways. There is also an excellent practice facility.

81. COUNTRY CLUB OF MOUNT DORA   CENTRAL REGION

1900 Country Club Blvd., Mount Dora
904-735-2263; Par: 72; Yards: 6,612–5,117.
Access: Open to the public. Green fees: Under $45.

A new Lloyd Clifton design that meanders through great oak and pine trees. Course is in great shape, with well-manicured greens. Most of them are surrounded by bunkers.

There are great lake views from 14 of the 18 holes. And when you are not admiring it, you better be careful of hitting into the water. On No. 18, the signature hole, your approach must carry water to a circular green surrounded by four traps and huge pines in the back.

82. OCEAN COURSE,
PONTE VEDRA INN AND CLUB   NORTHEAST REGION

200 Ponte Vedra Blvd., Ponte Vedra Beach
904-285-1111; Par: 72; Yards: 6,515–5,230.
Access: Open to the public; Green fees: $50 to $100.

A wonderful old Robert Trent Jones layout that boasts the world's first island green, the course is nestled in the charming Ponte Vedra Beach community. Five minutes away from Florida's top-ranked course (TPC–Sawgrass), the Ocean Course was slated to host the 1945 Ryder Cup matches that were called off because of World War II.

The course is a lot of fun to play, with blind tee shots over fairway bunkers, several severe doglegs, elevated greens and lots of water. The ninth hole is the island par 3, but this one is much larger than its more famous neighbor at TPC–Sawgrass.

83. GOLD COURSE, DORAL RESORT   SOUTHEAST REGION

4400 NW 87th Ave., Miami
305-592-2000—Resort; Par: 70; Yards: 6,361–5,422.
Availability: Public, discount for resort guests.
Green fees: $25 to $100.

The second-best course in Doral's four-course resort, the Gold underwent a renovation guided by PGA professional Raymond Floyd in late 1994 and early 1995. Call for availability. The course should get better and tougher. With water in play on almost every hole, distance isn't the issue, location is.

Everyone knows about No. 18, a par 4 with an island green, but there is plenty of water on the rest of the course. On the par 4 No. 10, for example, you must carry water on both your tee shot and your approach shot. You do not have to stay at the resort to play the course, but resort guests get a discount and you can reserve your tee time further in advance.

84. PALMER COURSE,
SADDLEBROOK RESORT   SOUTHWEST REGION

5700 Saddlebrook Way, Wesley Chapel
813-973-1111; Par: 71; Yards: 6,469–5,212.
Access: Open to the public, discount for resort guests.
Green fees: $30–$115.

Shorter than the Saddlebrook Course also at the resort, the newer Palmer Course places a higher demand on accuracy. There is water everywhere. No. 1 is a perfect example: Your tee shot is over water to a narrow fairway that tails right to a green with water on the left.

No. 5 is a nice par 4 with water in front and to the right of the bulkheaded green. The course winds around several lakes and because it is not very long, it is the water and narrow fairways that give the course its bite.

85. PONCE DE LEON
GOLF & CONFERENCE RESORT   NORTHEAST REGION

4000 U.S. Highway 1 North, St. Augustine
904-829-5314; Par: 72; Yards: 6,878–5,315.
Access: Open to the public; Green fees: $50–$100.

In the oldest Florida city is one of the oldest courses to make the Top 100. Legendary architect Donald Ross designed this course, one of the first in the state, in 1916 for guests of the Flagler family. The front nine is lined with live oaks and magnolia trees, while the back nine is a links-stye course and more wide open.

Water and wetlands come into play often. The course has been faithfully maintained and is in very good shape.

86. EAST COURSE, BONAVENTURE RESORT

200 Bonaventure Blvd., Ft. Lauderdale   SOUTHEAST REGION
305-389-2100. Par: 72; Yards: 7,011–5,304.
Access: Open to the public; Green fees: Under $40.

It's hard to block out the water you must carry on the par 3 third hole—because you can hear it. The green is elevated and the front of the green is a waterfall. It's only 160 yards from the back tees and bunkers guard the back of the green.

The course is long and flat, with lots of water and sand. Water comes into play on 14 of the holes. It is usually in good shape and one of the most popular places in Ft. Lauderdale.

87. SANDPIPER COURSE, INNISBROOK RESORT   SOUTHWEST REGION

U.S. Highway 19 South, Tarpon Springs
813-942-2000;
27 holes—Par: 35/35/35; Yards: 3,002/2,967/3,243.
Access: Resort guest only. Green fees: $50 and up.

The shortest of the three great courses at Innisbrook Resort, Sandpiper is really three nines that can be interchanged. There is water and trouble everywhere. It is the toughest short course you will play. Guests usually play this course first before moving on to the Island and Copperhead.

Because there is no room for error, you may want to keep your driver in the bag and hit 3-wood or long irons off the tee. Like prime real estate, this course is all about location, location, location.

88. PALISADES COUNTRY CLUB   CENTRAL REGION

16510 Palisades Blvd., Clermont
904-394-0085; Par: 72; Yards: 6,988–5,537.
Access: Open to the public; Green fees: Under $50.

Another one of Joe Lee's fine designs (Diamondback, Golf Club of Marco), Palisades has some of the hilliest land in Central Florida. Once you get past the spartan clubhouse and meandering road through the residential development, the course is worth the trip.

There are bulkheaded greens which are tough to putt and rolling fairways. Panelist Kenny Winn (Falcon's Fire golf professional) praised the course's design and layout.

89. HUNTINGTON HILLS COUNTRY CLUB   CENTRAL REGION

2626 Duff Road, Lakeland
813-859-3689; Par: 72; Yards: 6,679–5,129.
Access: Open to the public; Green fees: Under $50.

The best daily-fee course in Lakeland, Huntington Hills is a Ron Garl design that uses little water. A links-style course with rolling fairways and some unusual holes, the challenging layout features elevated tees, a double green, large bunkers. and a short par with a huge hill blocking your view of the green.

Always in good shape and a bargain most of the year, the course is popular with local players. One of the best holes is No. 3 (par 4, 423 yards). Your tee shot is to a wide fairway, but your approach a lake to a smallish green.

90. ISLANDSIDE COURSE, LONGBOAT KEY CLUB SOUTHWEST REGION

301 Gulf of Mexico Dr., Longboat Key
813-383-9571; 72; Yards: 6,792–5,198.
Access: Resort guests only. Green fees: $50 and up.

There is water everywhere—literally. On every hole. Like on No. 2, a par 5 with water surrounding the green to the right, to the left and in front. There are hundreds of palm trees, which are pretty, but do nothing to stop the wind when it blows off the Gulf of Mexico, which is often.

There are also plenty of bunkers. The result is one really tough golf course. Bring extra golf balls.

91. RIVER HILLS SOUTHWEST REGION

3943 New River Hills Parkway, Valrico
813-653-3323; Par: 72; Yards: 7,004–5,253.
Access: Open to the public weekdays, after noon on weekends.
Green fees: Under $75.

This is a great place to get the feel of playing in a private club. It is part of an Arvida residential community with many members; the course is set up for them. A Joe Lee design that is built around lakes, the course has a wide-open feel and playability. Live oaks dot the course, which stretches to more than 7,000 yards from the back tees.

No. 6 is a good par 5 with water on both sides of the fairway and a river cutting across the fairway. Depending on how you hit your drive, you can hit over the river on the second shot or lay up and have a longer approach to a green guarded by bunkers.

92. WESTCHESTER GOLF &
COUNTRY CLUB   SOUTHEAST REGION

12250 Westchester Club Dr., Boyton Beach
407-734-6300—Public—Par: 72; Yards: 6,760–4,886.
Access: Public; Green fees: $25 to $75.

Bring lots of golf balls. There is water on almost every hole of this
Karl Litten design. The first hole sets the tone: a par 5 that doglegs 90
degrees to the right after the tee shot. That tee shot is over water. The
fairway rises, then falls to a well-bunkered green. But don't get in-
timidated by the water; the greens are large and it is a lot of fun to
play here. The course is always in excellent shape and offers great
deals in the summer. There is also a lighted par 3 course that is
among the best in the state.

93. RIVER CLUB   SOUTHWEST REGION

6600 River Club Rd., Bradenton
813-751-4211; Par: 72; Yards: 7,026–5,157.
Access: Open to the public; Green fees: Under $50.

If this course doesn't get completely ruined by houses lining the
fairways—they already crowd the front side—this will continue to
be a good course. Ron Garl used lots of water to toughen up this
course. And when there isn't water, such as on the par 3 No. 15, the
green is almost completely surrounded by sand.

The back nine is more scenic, especially No. 16, a long par 4 (416
yards from the back) to an almost island green.

94. SOUTH COURSE, GRENELEFE
GOLF & TENNIS RESORT   CENTRAL REGION

3200 S.R. 546, Haines City
813-422-7511; Par 71; Yards: 6,869–5,174.
Access: Open to the public; Green fees: $50 to $99.

The second of three courses to open at the resort, Ron Garl collaborated with PGA player Andy Bean to craft a challenging course
with lots of sand and rolling fairways. There are holes with fairways
that run almost the entire length of the hole, a double dogleg par 5
and lots of mounding.

95. CAROLINA CLUB SOUTHEAST REGION

3011 Rock Island Rd., Margate
305-753-4000; Par: 71; Yards: 6,550–6,101.
Access: Public; Green fees: $50 to $100.

Upscale public course with great clubhouse and well maintained facility. Course is tight, with water on 17 holes. Run by same folks who oversee Deer Creek, one of Florida's Top 50.

96. HOMBRE GOLF CLUB NORTHWEST REGION

120 Coyote Pass, Panama City Beach
904-234-3673. Par: 72. Yards: 6,820–4,800.
Access: Open to the public. Green fees: $40-$75.

Only a 3-wood away from the beaches, Hombre is a lot tougher than it initially appears. Tight and with water a factor on 15 of the 18 holes, Hombre hosted PGA Nike Tour events in 1994 and 1995. The course demands you to be accurate and fairly long off the tee.

The second hole is a 457-yard par 4 and No. 7 features an island green. The course has an excellent practice area and a nice clubhouse on a hill.

97. MIAMI SHORES COUNTRY CLUB SOUTHEAST REGION

10000 Biscayne Blvd., Miami Shores
305-795-2366; Par: 72; Yards: 6,455–5,651.
Access: Open to the public; Green fees: Under $50.

Small elevated greens, most well-bunkered, provide the challenge on this course built in the 1930s. No. 9, a tough par 4, measures 425 yards from the back and plays to an elevated green. There is room in the fairways to spray it a little, but you really need to get on the right side of the green to score well.

98. BUFFALO CREEK SOUTHWEST REGION

8100 Erie Rd., Palmetto
813-776-2611; Par: 72; Yards: 7,005—5,261
Access: Open to the public; Green fees: Under $40.

Yet another Ron Garl design in Southwest Florida, this one is not as well known as some of his others, but is just as good. Rolling fairways, large bunkers and bulkheaded greens make this a beautiful and challenging course. This is also one of the best deals in the state.

99. THE DUNES, SANIBEL

949 Sand Castle Road, Sanibel Island
813-472-2535; Par: 70; Yards: 5,715–4,100.
Access: Open to the public; Green fees: $30 to $90.

Don't say we didn't warn you: don't be fooled by the length. It is tougher than it looks. Water comes into play on every hole. The course is very scenic, winding through wetlands and protected areas that will never be developed.

You need to hit your irons well here. Most of the greens have forced carries over water, or there is water on both sides of the fairway. The course closed from May to November 1995 to rebuild the greens and fairways.

100. CLUB MEADOWS,
MARRIOTT'S BAY POINT RESORT

100 Delwood Beach Road, Panama City Beach
904-235-6909; Par: 72; Yards: 6,913–4,999.
Access: Open to the public; Green fees: $50 to $100.

Much, much more wide open than its sister course Lagoon Legend (one of the hardest courses in the state), Club Meadows is often overlooked by golfers determined to tackle the tougher course. Club Meadows is more inviting. There are not as many forced carries—No. 18 however is a tricky dogleg with water right of the green—and there are few surprises.

The course is in good shape and not as crowded as Lagoon Legend. It's a good place to warm up for the monster next door.

COURSES BY REGION
A DIRECTORY OF THE TOP 100 COURSES IN EACH REGION AND OTHER NOTABLE COURSES

SOUTHEAST REGION

This region boasts 23 of the Top 100 courses in the state. Summaries of each of these courses follow; you'll find more detailed information about them in the Top 100 section of this book.

Three of the top four courses in the region host PGA or Senior PGA Tour events. Many of the others could, too, and some used to. They all have plenty of water and all are affected by the wind.

But to draw similarities between them would take away from the unique qualities that got them on the Top 100 list.

Additionally, there are 16 courses in the area that didn't make the Top 100, but are worth playing if you're in the neighborhood.

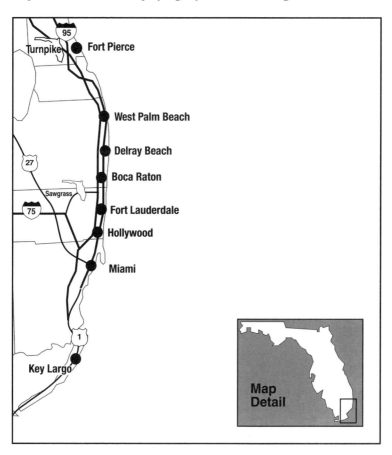

COURSES IN THE TOP 100

These courses made the list of the Top 100 courses in the state. You'll find more information about them under their respective listings in the top 100 section of this book.

7 LINKS AT KEY BISCAYNE

6700 Crandon Blvd., Key Biscayne
(305) 361-9139; Par: 72; Yards: 7,070–5,690.
Access: Open to the public; Green fees: Under $50

The best municipal course in Florida. Site of Senior PGA Tour event.

8 BLUE COURSE, DORAL RESORT

4400 NW 87th Ave., Miami
(305) 592-2000; Par: 72; Yards: 6,939–5,784.
Access: Open to the public; discount for resort guests;
Green fees: $25 to $125.

Features a famous finishing hole. Site of PGA Tour event.

10 EMERALD DUNES

2100 Emerald Dunes Dr., West Palm Beach
(407) 684-GOLF; Par: 72; Yards: 7,006–4,676.
Access: Open to the public; Green fees: $40 to $125.

A Tom Fazio masterpiece with a massive dune as the focal point.

15 CHAMPIONS COURSE, PGA NATIONAL

1000 Avenue of Champions, Palm Beach Gardens
(407) 627-1800; Par: 72; Yards: 7,022–5,377.
Access: Resort guests only; Green fees: $100 and up.

Jack Nicklaus redesigned the course. Site of Senior PGA Championship.

25 SOUTH COURSE, TURNBERRY ISLE RESORT

19999 W. Country Club Drive, North Miami Beach
(305) 932-6200; Par: 72; Yards: 7,003–5,581
Access: Resort guests only; Green fees: $50 to $95.

Tough, elegant resort with two Robert Trent Jones courses.

The 18th green at Deer Creek, which renowned architect Arthur Hills recently reconstructed from the ground up.

29 WEST COURSE, GOLF CLUB OF MIAMI

6801 Miami Gardens Dr., Miami
(305) 829-8456; Par: 72; Yards: 7,017–5,298.
Access: Open to the public; Green fees: Under $50.

Demanding, tournament-quality course. Jackie Gleason used to have a home on the course.

30 DEER CREEK GOLF CLUB

2801 Country Club Blvd., Deerfield Beach
(305) 421-5550; Par: 72; Yards: 7,038–5319.
Access: Open to the public; Green fees: $50 to $100.

Arthur Hills recently renovated the course. Always in excellent condition.

33 SILVER COURSE, DORAL PARK

5001 NW 104th Ave.
(305) 594-0954; Par: 70; Yards: 6,801–5,064
Access: Open to the public; Green fees: $25 to $75.

Mounding, island par 3 make this a challenging course.

35 EMERALD HILLS

4100 North Hills Drive, Hollywood
(305) 961-4000; Par: 72; Yards: 7,003–5,032
Access: Open to the public; Green fees: Under $75.

Water comes into play often and two excellent par 5s have water in front of the greens.

50 BILTMORE GOLF CLUB

1210 Anastasia Ave., Coral Gables
(305) 460-5366; Par: 71; Yards: 6,652–55,697.
Access: Open to the public; Green fees: Under $40.

This classic Donald Ross design is the oldest course in Top 50. Opened in 1926.

57 CHAMPIONS CLUB AT SUMMERFIELD

3400 S.E. Summerfield Way, Stuart
407-283-1500. Par: 72. Yards: 6,809–5,614.
Access: Open to the public; Green fees: Under $75.

A new Tom Fazio design through wetlands.

61 BREAKERS WEST

1550 Flagler Parkway, West Palm Beach
407-790-7000. Par: 71. Yards: 6,901–5,385.
Access: Resort guests only. Green fees: $50 to $100.

Back nine has been renovated and new staff has upgraded the course's condition.

64 POLO TRACE

13397 Hagen Ranch Road, Delray Beach
407-495-5301. Par: 72; Yards: 7,096–5,314.
Access: Open to the public; Green fees: $50 to $100.

A Scottish-links style course with some water.

68 CYPRESS COURSE, PALM BEACH POLO & COUNTRY CLUB

11809 Polo Club Rd., West Palm Beach
407-798-7401. Par: 72 Yards: 7,116–5,172.
Access: Resort guests only after noon every day.
Green fees: $50 to $100.

A rare Pete Dye course in South Florida. Very popular in the winter.

69 BINKS FOREST

400 Binks Drive, Wellington
407-795-0028. Par: 72; Yards: 7,091–5,468.
Access: Open to the public; Green fees: $50 to $100.

An excellent course that used to be private. It features tree-lined fairways.

75 COLONY WEST

6800 NW 88th Ave., Tamarac
305-726-8430. Par: 72; Yards: 7,271–5,422.
Access: Open to the public; Green fees: Under $50.

One of the longest courses in South Florida.

77 DUNES COURSE, PALM BEACH POLO & COUNTRY CLUB

11809 Polo Club Rd., West Palm Beach
407-798-7401. Par: 72 Yards: 7,050–5,516.
Access: Resort guests only; Green fees: $50 to $100.

A Ron Garl design with water on 16 holes.

79 EAST COURSE, GOLF CLUB OF MIAMI

6801 Miami Gardens Dr., Country Club of Miami
305-829-4700 - Public; Par: 70; Yards: 6,353–5,025.
Access: Open to the public; Green fees: Under $50.

Some of the best greens in the region and a good collection of par 3s.

83 GOLD COURSE, DORAL RESORT

4400 NW 87th Ave., Miami
305-592-2000 - Resort; Par: 70; Yards: 6,361–5,422.
Availability: Public, discount for resort guests.
Green fees: $25 to $100.

Second-best course at Doral Resort after Blue Monster. No. 18 is a par 4 with an island green.

86 EAST COURSE, BONAVENTURE RESORT

200 Bonaventure Blvd., Ft. Lauderdale
305-389-2100. Par: 72; Yards: 7,011–5,304.
Access: Open to the public; Green fees: Under $40.

Signature hole is a par 3 that calls for a tee shot over a waterfall.

92 WESTCHESTER GOLF & COUNTRY CLUB

12250 Westchester Club Dr., Boyton Beach
407-734-6300 - Public - Par: 72; Yards: 6,760–4,886.
Access: Public; Green fees: $25 to $75.

Lots of water and doglegs, but plenty of room to get around.

95 CAROLINA CLUB

3011 Rock Island Rd., Margate
305-753-4000; Par: 71; Yards: 6,550–6,101.
Access: Public; Green fees: $50 to $100.

Tight course that is well-maintained and has excellent service and amenities.

97 MIAMI SHORES COUNTRY CLUB

10000 Biscayne Blvd., Miami Shores
305-795-2366; Par: 72; Yards: 6,455–5,651.
Access: Open to the public; Green fees: Under $50.

Classic course with small, elevated greens.

OTHER NOTABLE COURSES
IN THE SOUTHEAST FLORIDA REGION

These courses didn't make the Top 100, but they're worth playing if you're in the area.

(Listed alphabetically)

ATLANTIS COUNTRY CLUB

190 Atlantis Blvd., West Palm Beach
407-965-7700; Par 72; Yards: 6,477–5,258.
Access: Public; Green fees: $25 to $75.

An old-style course with many of the fairways lined with trees. Always in very good shape.

CALIFORNIA CLUB

20898 San Simeon Way, North Miami Beach
305-651-3590; Par: 72; Yards: 6,670–5,675.
Access: Public after noon every day; Green fees: Under $50.

Very little water and some dramatic doglegs. Highlight is the final three holes which wrap around a lake. Greens redone in 1994.

DON SHULA'S HOTEL AND GOLF CLUB

15255 Bull Run Rd., Miami Lakes
305-821-1150; Par 72; Yards: 7,055–5,639.
Access: Public, discount for resort guests; Green fees: $45 to $70.

A course that is old-fashioned and no-nonsense, just like Miami Dolphins Coach Don Shula, who has an interest in the place. Many of the greens are elevated and the course was maintained better in 1995 than in previous years.

DORAL RESORT, RED COURSE

4400 NW 87th Ave., Miami
305-592-2000; Par: 71; Yards: 6,210–5,254.
Access: Public, discount for resort guests; Green fees: $25 to $100.

Lots of water, lots of doglegs, but not very long. If you keep it straight, you will score well here. Not as good as Doral's Blue and Gold, but far better than the White.

FAIRWINDS GOLF COURSE

4400 Fairwinds Dr., Ft. Pierce
407-462-4653; Par: 72; Yards: 6,783–5,392.
Access: Public; Green fees: Under $35.

A very playable course, one that increases your confidence. No. 18 is a nice dogleg left around water to an elevated green.

GOLF CLUB OF MIAMI, SOUTH COURSE

6801 Miami Gardens Dr., Country Club of Miami
305-829-4700; Par: 62; Yards: 4,240–3,281.
Access: Public; Green fees: Under $25.

Don't let the par 62 fool you; this is a good golf test and the course is always in better shape than most regulation length courses. There are 8 par 4s and 10 par 3s that demand precise shots.

GRAND PALMS GOLF & COUNTRY CLUB

110 Grand Palms Dr., Pembroke Pines
305-437-3334; Par: 35/37/36; Yards: Grand—3,337–2,571;
Royal—3,420–2,674; Sable—3,316–2,978.
Access: Open to the public; Green fees: Under $50.

A well-maintained course that requires accuracy because of all the water. The Sable nine opened in 1994.

JACARANDA GOLF CLUB, EAST AND WEST COURSES

9200 W. Broward Blvd., Plantation
305-472-5855; Par: 72; Yards: 7,170–5,668 (East);
6,729–5,314 (West).
Access: Public; Green fees: $25 to $60.

The excellent greens are what make these courses. Both courses are traditional Florida courses, each with water on 16 of the 18 holes. Panelist Guy Boros, a PGA Tour player who grew up in South Florida, listed the East Course as one of his favorites. "Good driving course," he said.

KEY WEST GOLF CLUB

6450 College Road, Key West
305-294-5232; Par 70; Yards: 6,526–5,183.
Access: Public; Green fees: Under $50.

This course is notable because of where it is. It's the only course in Key West; the nearest course you can play is 100 miles away in Homestead.

PGA NATIONAL GOLF CLUB

400 Avenue of Champions, Palm Beach Gardens
407-627-1800; Three courses, each par 72.
Access: Resort guests only; Green fees: $50 to $100.

Haig Course: Best of the three other courses at PGA National (Champions Course one of Florida's Top 50); an early Tom Fazio design.

General Course: A tough long course with some forced carries onto the greens.

Squire Course: The shortest of the resort's courses and the one with the most water.

PRESIDENTIAL COUNTRY CLUB

19650 NE 18th Ave., North Miami Beach
305-932-8740; Par: 72; Yards: 6,964–5,794
Access: Public; Green fees: Under $50.

A charming, old course with huge oaks and ficus trees lining the fairways. Site of an old PGA Tour stop. Arnold Palmer set the course record (62). Conditioning has improved in the past year.

ST. LUCIE WEST COUNTRY CLUB

951 SW Country Club Dr., Port St. Lucie
407-340-1911; Par: 72; Yards: 6,901–5,054
Access: Public; Green fees: Under $50.

Not terribly long, but you must keep the ball in play. Excellent service and very friendly staff.

SANDRIDGE GOLF CLUB, DUNES AND LAKES COURSES

5300 73rd St., Vero Beach
407-770-5000; Both courses par 72.
Access: Public; Green fees: Under $50.

Dunes Course (yards: 6,817–4,944) features nice rolling fairways cut out of the wetlands and is longer than the Lakes Course.

Lakes (yards: 6,138–4,625), no surprise, has a lot of water.

TURNBERRY ISLE RESORT & CLUB, NORTH COURSE

19999 W. Country Club Dr., North Miami Beach
305-932-6200; Resort; Par: 70; Yards: 6,323–5,589.
Access: Resort guests only; Green fees: $50 to $100.

A finely maintained Robert Trent Jones layout, the North Course is just as picturesque as the more famous South Course. The North Course is sneaky tough, with water in play on 10 holes and well-bunkered greens that require high approaches. No. 5, a 562-yard par 5 has water all along the right side of the fairway and the elevated green sticks out into the lake, calling for an approach over water.

WEST PALM BEACH COUNTRY CLUB

7001 Parker Ave., West Palm Beach
407-582-2019; Public; Par: 72; Yards: 6,789–5,884.
Access: Public; Green fees: Under $50.

A classic Dick Wilson design, the course opened in 1947 and is one of the best municipal courses in Southeast Florida. A favorite among locals, the course is in very good shape for the amount of play it gets. One thing about the course is different from every other one in Southeast Florida—there is no water that comes into play. Every green is elevated and the bunkers are deep. There are some mild elevation changes—and combined with the elevated greens—that make the course play longer than it looks.

WINSTON TRAILS

6101 Winston Trails Blvd., Lake Worth
407-439-3700; Par: 72; Yards: 6,820–5,378.
Access: Public; Green fees: $50 to $100.

The Joe Lee designed course opened in 1993 and there is water on 15 holes and lots of dogleg rights (four on the back nine). No. 17 is an island par 3.

SOUTHWEST REGION

If you love golf, it could take you a month to drive the 100 miles between Naples and Tampa. There are so many good courses, all in such good condition, that finding one to play anywhere in the region will not take long.

From the hills of Innisbrook to the nature preserve surrounding Sanibel's The Dunes, most of these courses also provide an excellent setting for your round.

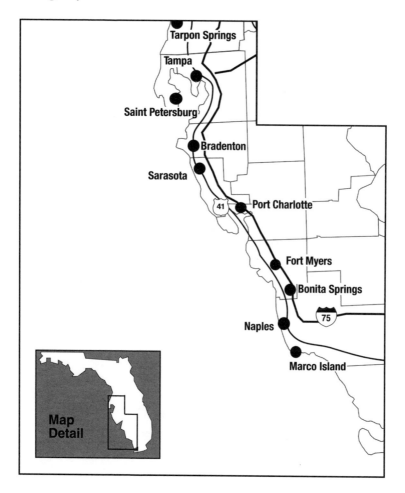

COURSES IN THE TOP 100

These courses made the list of the Top 100 courses in the state. You'll find more information about them under their respective listings in the top 100 section of this book.

2   COPPERHEAD, INNISBROOK HILTON RESORT

P.O. Box 1088, Tarpon Springs
813-942-2000; Par: 72; Yards: 7,087–5,506.
Access: Innisbrook resort guests only;
Green fees: $100 and up.

Everything you could want is here: elevation changes, tournament conditions, serene setting and excellent amenities.

11   PELICAN'S NEST

4450 Pelican's Nest Dr., Bonita Springs
(813) 947-4600; Par: 36/36/36/36.
Yards: Hurricane—3,458–2,511; Gator—3,558; 2,690.
Seminole—3,514–2,615; Panther—3,461–2,534.
Access: Open to the public; Green fees: Under $75.

A must-play course in the region, this Tom Fazio layout winds through mangroves and is immaculately maintained.

22   TPC–TAMPA BAY

5100 Terrain de Golf Dr., Lutz
(813) 671-3311; Par: 71; Yards: 6,898–6,008.
Access: Open to the public; Green fees: $50 to $100.

The greens make this course tough. Home of a Senior PGA Tour event.

23   BLOOMINGDALE GOLFERS CLUB

1802 Nature's Way Blvd., Valrico
(813) 685-4105; Par: 72; Yards: 7,165-5,506
Access: Open to the public Monday through Thursday and Friday until noon. Green fees: $50 to $75.

A fabulous layout in a secluded setting, this is a no-nonsense hangout for the golf purist.

24 EASTWOOD GOLF CLUB

4600 Bruce Herd Lane, Ft. Myers
(813) 275-4848; Par: 72; Yards: 6,772–5,116.
Access: Open to the public; Green fees: Under $40.

Overall, the most impressive municipal facility in the state. Great course in a great setting.

27 ISLAND COURSE, INNISBROOK HILTON RESORT

U.S. highway 19 South, Tarpon Springs
(813) 942-2000; Par: 72; Yards: 6,999–5,892.
Access: Resort guests only; Green fees: $50 to $90.

An excellent, tight layout through tall, tree-lined fairways that demands accurate shots.

28 LELY FLAMINGO

8004 Lely Resort Blvd., Naples
(813) 793-2223; Par: 72; Yards: 7,171–5,377.
Access: Open to the public; Green fees: $40 to $95.

A wonderful, water-laden beauty with rock-lined greens.

You've heard of island greens. The Flamingo Course at Lely features an island *hole*, No. 5.

39 FOX HOLLOW GOLF CLUB

10050 Robert Trent Jones Parkway, Odessa
(813) 376-6333; Par: 72; Yards: 7,138–4,454.
Access: Open to the public; Green fees: Under $60.

A new course just north of Tampa, it has lots of sand and several holes that cut into a forest.

40 GATEWAY GOLF CLUB

11360 Championship Dr., Ft. Myers
(813) 561-1010; Par: 72; Yards: 6,974–5,323.
Access: Open to the public; Green fees: $30 to $90.

Tom Fazio created two nines in one here: a links-style layout with few trees on the front and Carolina-style on the back.

55 WESTCHASE

10307 Radcliffe Dr., Tampa
813-854-2331; Par: 72; Yards: 6,710–5,205.
Access: Open to the public; Green fees: $25 to $45.

This Lloyd Clifton designed course is well-maintained and in a wooded setting.

56 SADDLEBROOK COURSE, SADDLEBROOK RESORT

5700 Saddlebrook Way, Wesley Chapel
813-973-1111; Par: 70; Yards: 6,603–5,183.
Access: Open to the public, discount for resort guests.
Green fees: $30 to $115.

The original course at the resort, it was designed by Arnold Palmer.

60 UNIVERSITY PARK COUNTRY CLUB

7671 University Park Blvd., Sarasota
813-359-9999; Par: 72; Yards: 6,951–4,914.
Access: Open to the public; Green fees: $40 to $85.

Among the best conditioned courses in the region, this Ron Garl layout has some excellent holes.

62 NAPLES BEACH HOTEL & GOLF CLUB

851 Gulf Shore Blvd. North, Naples
813-261-2222; Par: 72; Yards: 6,497–5,267.
Access: Open to the public, discount to hotel guests.
Green fees: Under $75.

Across the street from the ocean, this is a classic course that is fun to play.

66 GOLF CLUB OF MARCO

400 S. Collier Boulevard, Marco Island
813-793-6060; Par: 72; Yards: 6,898–5,416.
Access: Open to the public; Green fees: $35 to $90.

Lots of water and several bulkheaded greens define this course.

73 OLDE HICKORY GOLF & COUNTRY CLUB

14670 Olde Hickory Blvd., Ft. Myers
813-768-3335; Par: 72; Yards: 6,601–5,005.
Access: Open to the public; Green fees: Under $50.

This Ron Garl course winds through a residential neighborhood and has an island green par 3.

84 PALMER COURSE, SADDLEBROOK RESORT

5700 Saddlebrook Way, Wesley Chapel
813-973-1111; Par: 71; Yards: 6,469–5,212.
Access: Open to the public, discount for resort guests.
Green fees: $30 to $115.

The course is short, but with lots of water. The setting is very nice.

87 SANDPIPER COURSE, INNISBROOK HILTON RESORT

U.S. Highway 19 South, Tarpon Springs
813-942-2000; 27 holes—Par: 35/35/35.
Yards: 3,002/2,967/3,243.
Access: Resort guest only. Green fees: $50 and up.

Three nines that are not long, but with plenty of water and tree-lined fairways.

90 ISLANDSIDE COURSE, LONGBOAT KEY CLUB

301 Gulf of Mexico Dr., Longboat Key
813-383-9571; 72; Yards: 6,792–5,198.
Access: Resort guests only. Green fees: $50 and up.

Fairly wide-open fairways dotted with palm trees.

91 RIVER HILLS

3943 New River Hills Parkway, Valrico
813-653-3323; Par: 72; Yards: 7,004–5,253.
Access: Open to the public weekdays, after noon on weekends.
Green fees: Under $75.

This is a private club that opens up to the public; service is great, course is flat and landing areas generous.

93 THE RIVER CLUB

6600 River Club Rd., Bradenton
813-751-4211; Par: 72; Yards: 7,026–5,157.
Access: Open to the public; Green fees: Under $50.

The secluded, and yet undeveloped, setting around the back nine give this course its charm.

98 BUFFALO CREEK

8100 Erie Rd., Palmetto
813-776-2611; Par: 72; Yards:
Access: Open to the public; Green fees: Under $40.

A hidden gem, this Ron Garl layout is always in good shape and one of the best deals in Florida.

99 THE DUNES

949 Sand Castle Road, Sanibel Island
813-472-2535; Par: 70; Yards: 5,715–4,100.
Access: Open to the public; Green fees: $30 to $90.

A personal favorite, this course is short and with lots of water, but it is not overbearing and its setting is wonderful.

OTHER NOTABLE COURSES
IN THE SOUTHWEST FLORIDA REGION

These courses didn't make the Top 100, but they're worth playing if you're in the area.

(Listed alphabetically)

BARDMOOR NORTH GOLF CLUB

7919 Bardmoor Blvd., Largo
813-397-0483; Par: 72; Yards: 6,950–5,569.
Access: Public; Green fees: $25 to $60.

The course recently has improved practice areas and course conditions. A good layout with many elevated greens.

BEACHVIEW GOLF CLUB

1100 Par View Drive, Sanibel
813-472-2626; Par: 71; Yards: 6,137–4,737.
Access: Open to the public; Green fees: Under $50 to $100.

A nine-course for many years, the back nine was added in 1993. There is water on every hole on the back nine, including in front of the green on the short par 4 No. 16.

BELLEVIEW MIDO COUNTRY CLUB

1501 Indian Rocks Road, Belleair
813-581-5498; Par: 72; Yards: 6,655–5,703.
Access: Open to the public; Green fees: Under $50.

Owned by the majestic and historic Belleview Mido Hotel, this Donald Ross layout is wide open and has many elevated greens.

CALUSA LAKES GOLF COURSE

1995 Calusa Lakes Blvd., Nokomis
813-484-8996; Par: 36/36/36; Yards: 3,404/3,349/3,330.
Access: Open to the public; Green fees: Under $50.

Carved out of a heavily wooded site, Calusa Lakes winds through a development where the homes do not crowd the course.

CORAL OAKS

1800 NW 28th Ave., Cape Coral
813-283-4100; Par: 72; Yards: 6,623–4,803.
Access: Open to the public; Green fees: Under $50.

An excellent Arthur Hills layout that winds through tall pines,
Coral Oaks has some of the best rates in the region during the summer. Only drawback is that conditioning is not consistent.

EAGLES GOLF CLUB

16101 Nine Eagles Dr., Odessa
813-920-6681; Par: 36/36/36; Yards: 3,504–3,564–3,630.
Access: Open to the public; Green fees: Under $50.

The three nines are cut out of a large cypress forest. The forest
has the most of its namesake and is the most popular. The Lakes
and Oaks nines have large elevated greens and lots of water and
bunkers.

FT. MYERS COUNTRY CLUB

3591 McGregor, Blvd., Ft. Myers
813-936-2457; Par: 71; Yards: 6,414-5,135.
Access: Open to the public; Green fees: Open to the public.

A Donald Ross classic, this course is operated by the city of Ft.
Myers, the same folks who run the magnificent Eastwood Golf Club
(No. 24). Walking is allowed any time.

FOXFIRE GOLF CLUB

7200 Proctor Rd., Sarasota
813-921-7757; Par: 36/36/36; Yards: 3,017–3,196–3,084.
Access: Open to the public; Green fees: Under $50.

A fine course with no houses lining the fairways and three nines
that add variety. Holes wind through forest and wetlands.

HUNTER'S RIDGE COUNTRY CLUB

12500 Hunter's Ridge, Bonita Springs
813-992-7667; Par: 72; Yards: 6,317–4,154.

A shot-maker's course with water around many greens, including the island No. 18. Length is not an issue, but location certainly
is; water comes into play on 17 holes.

LOCHMOOR COUNTRY CLUB

3911 Orange Grove Blvd., Fort Myers
813-995-0501; Par: 72; Yards: 6,901–5,152.
Access: Open to the public; Green fees: Under $50.

A long, wide-open course tailor-made for those who like to bomb away with the driver. Many greens accept bump-and-run shots.

OAK FORD GOLF CLUB

1552 Palm View Rd., Sarasota
813-371-3680; Par: 72; yards: 6,734–5,814.
Access: Open to the public; Green fees: Under $50.

Another Ron Garl design in the region. His signature long, winding bunkers and bulkheaded greens rising from the sand are all here.

PALM RIVER

331 Palm River Dr., Naples
813-597-6082; Par: 72; Yards: 6,718–5,716.
Access: Open to the public; Green fees: Under $40.

One of the oldest courses in Naples, Palm River has been steadily upgraded during the past couple of years. The course has plenty of water and fairways dotted with palm trees.

ROSEDALE GOLF & COUNTRY CLUB

5100 87th St., Bradenton
813-756-0004; Par: 72; Yards: 6,779–5,169.
Access: Open to the public; Green fees: Under $50.

A tight, tight course with water lining many holes and trees around many greens. You may not even want to bring your driver.

TATUM RIDGE GOLF LINKS

421 North Tatum Road, Sarasota
813-378-4211; Par: 72; Yards: 6,757–5,149;
Access: Open to the public; Green fees: Under $50.

A Scottish-style links course that incorporates wetlands and 11 lakes throughout the layout. There is also a good practice facility.

CENTRAL REGION

This is the richest region in Florida for excellent golf courses. There are great resorts, five courses (four in the Top 100) at Walt Disney World alone, and first-rate daily fee courses.

The area also continues to grow and many of the courses that made the Top 100 are less than five years old. Sources say that even Disney World will build another course in the next three years.

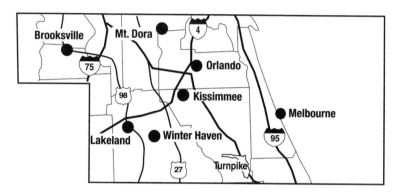

COURSES IN THE TOP 100

These courses made the list of the Top 100 courses in the state. You'll find more information about them under their respective listings in the top 100 section of this book.

3 PINE BARRENS, WORLD WOODS

17590 Ponce DeLeon Blvd., Brooksville
(904) 796-5500; Par: 71; Yards: 6,902–5,301.
Access: Open to the public; Green fees: $80 and up (for 36 holes, range balls).

Tom Fazio's best public-access course in Florida. There is nothing like it; has been compared to Pine Valley.

4 BAY HILL

9000 Bay Hill Blvd., Orlando
(407) 876-2429; Par: 72; Yards: 7,114–5,192.
Access: Lodge guests only; Green fees: $100 and up.

Arnold Palmer's winter home and site of PGA Tour event.

6 NORTH/SOUTH COURSE, GRAND CYPRESS

1 North Jacaranda, Orlando
(407) 239-4700; Par: 72; Yards: 6,993–5,328.
Access: Grand Cypress resort guests only; Green fees: $100 and up.

Jack Nicklaus did a great job creating a course from flat Florida land. A must play.

14 WEST COURSE, GRENELEFE RESORT

3200 S.R. 546, Haines City
(813) 422-7511; Par: 72; Yards: 7,325–5,398.
Access: Open to the public; Green fees: $50 to $99.

Long and tough, this course hosts many state tournaments. Good uphill and downhill holes.

17 GOLDEN OCALA

7300 U.S. Hwy. 27, Ocala
(904) 622-1098; Par: 72; Yards: 6,725–5,595.
Access: Open to the public; Green fees: Under $50.

Course has eight replica holes; you won't believe how good they are.

18 OSPREY RIDGE, WALT DISNEY WORLD

3451 Golf View, Lake Buena Vista
(407) 824-2270; Par: 72; Yards: 7,101–5,402.
Access: Open to the public; discount for resort guests.
Green fees: $40 to $100.

The best of the five courses at Disney World. Fazio did a nice job of not making it too tough.

20 NEW COURSE, GRAND CYPRESS RESORT

1 North Jacaranda, Orlando
(407) 239-4700; Par: 72; Yards: 6,773–5,314.
Access: Grand Cypress resort guests only; Green fees: $100 and up.

The best Scottish-style course in Florida. Jack Nicklaus included some re-creations of famous Scottish holes.

34 ROLLING OAKS, WORLD WOODS

17590 Ponce de Leon Blvd., Brooksville
(904) 796-5500; Par: 72; Yards: 6,985–5,245.
Access: Open to the public; Green fees: $40 and up.

Pine Barrens' sister course, it has more room and a more traditional design.

36 BAYTREE NATIONAL

8207 National Drive, Melbourne
(407) 259-9060; Par: 72; Yards: 7,043–4,803.
Access: Open to the public; Green fees: $27 to $68

A new Gary Player design with innovative use of red shale as a waste area.

37 METROWEST

2100 S. Hiawassee Road, Orlando
(407) 299-8800; Par: 72; Yards: 7,051–5,325.
Access: Open to the public; Green fees: $50 to $75.

A Robert Trent Jones Sr. design that has nice elevation changes and some tough holes.

Beauty and the Beast: The green at the 6th hole at Falcon's Fire is guarded by wetlands on the right

38 FALCON'S FIRE

3200 Seralago Blvd., Kissimmee
407-932-5007; Par: 72; Yards: 6,901–5,417.
Access: Open to the public; Green fees: $35 to $100.

A new Rees Jones layout very close to Disney World that is in excellent shape and has superb service.

45 DIAMONDBACK GOLF CLUB

6501 S.R. 544 East, Haines City
(813) 421-0437; Par: 72; Yards: 6,805–5,061
Access: Open to the public; Green fees: Under $50.

This course opened in 1995 and will be a great course. There is a waterfall from one fairway to another.

48 TIMACUAN GOLF & COUNTRY CLUB

550 Timacuan Blvd., Lake Mary
(407) 321-0010; Par: 72; Yards 7,019–5,401.
Access: Open to the public; Green fees: Under $60.

A hilly course just north of Orlando designed by Ron Garl.

52 EL CAMPEON, MISSION INN

10400 County Road 48, Howey-in-the-Hills
904-324-3101; Par: 72; Yards: 6,842–5,038.
Access: Open to the public, discount for resort guests.
Green fees: $50 to $100.

An old Florida course with lots of elevation changes, which is rare in Florida.

53 EAGLE PINES, WALT DISNEY WORLD

1 Vista Dr., Lake Buena Vista
904-824-2270; Par: 72; Yards: 6,772–4,838.
Access: Open to the public, discount for resort guests.
Green fees: $50 to $100.

Pete Dye's new creation at Disney, it is tight and low-key. A fun course.

59 EASTWOOD GOLF COURSE

13950 Golfway Blvd., Orlando
407-281-4653; Par: 72; Yards: 7,176–5,393.
Access: Open to the public. Green fees: Under $50.

The superb greens get all the attention, but there are some fine golf holes, too.

63 HUNTER'S CREEK

14401 Sports Club Way, Orlando
407-240-4653; Par: 72; Yards: 7,432–5,755.
Access: Open to the public. Green fees: Under $50 to $100.

One of the longest courses in Florida. There is also plenty of water.

70 SOUTHERN DUNES GOLF & COUNTRY CLUB

2888 Southern Dunes Blvd., Haines City
813-421-4653; Par: 72; Yards: 7,219–5,225.
Access: Open to the public. Green fees: Under $45.

Lots of sand and good mix of holes on this new course by up-and-coming architect Steve Smyers.

71 MAGNOLIA COURSE, WALT DISNEY WORLD

1 Magnolia Palm Dr., Lake Buena Vista
407-824-2270; Par 72; Yards: 6,957–5,398.
Access: Open to the public, discount for resort guests.
Green fees: $50 to $100.

Prettiest of the original three Disney courses. There is a par 3 with a bunker shaped like Mickey Mouse's ears.

72 PALM COURSE, WALT DISNEY WORLD

1 Magnolia Palm Dr., Lake Buena Vista
407-824-2270; Par: 72; Yards: 7,190–5,414.
Access: Open to the public, discount for resort guests.
Green fees: $50 to $100.

Longer and tougher to score on than neighboring Magnolia course.

76 HARBOR HILLS

6538 Lake Griffin Road, Lady Lake
904-753-7711; Par: 72; Yards: 6,878–5,355.
Access: Open to the public. Green fees: $25 to $45.

A quiet, out-of-the-way course with some hills.

78 OAKWOOD GOLF CLUB

1000 Capps Road, Lake Wales
813-676-8558; Par: 72; Yards: 6,891–5,216.
Access: Open to the public. Green fees: Under $35.

A hidden gem that is rarely crowded and located in a pristine, wooded setting.

81 COUNTRY CLUB OF MOUNT DORA

1900 Country Club Blvd., Mount Dora
904-735-2263; Par: 72; Yards: 6,612–5,117.
Access: Open to the public. Green fees: Under $45.

A new Lloyd Clifton design in a wonderful small town.

88 PALISADES COUNTRY CLUB

16510 Palisades Blvd., Clermont
904-394-0085; Par: 72; Yards: 6,988–5,537.
Access: Open to the public; Green fees: Under $50.

Another fine Joe Lee design that attracts golfers from Orlando because of its rolling terrain.

89 HUNTINGTON HILLS

2626 Duff Road, Lakeland
813-859-3689; Par: 72; Yards: 6,679–5,129.
Access: Open to the public; Green fees: Under $50.

The best course in Lakeland, this is links-style design by Ron Garl.

94 SOUTH COURSE, GRENELEFE GOLF & TENNIS RESORT

3200 S.R. 546, Haines City
813-422-7511; Par 71; Yards: 6,869–5,174.
Access: Open to the public; Green fees: $50 to $99.

A Ron Garl design with rolling fairways and lots of sand.

OTHER NOTABLE COURSES IN THE CENTRAL FLORIDA REGION

These courses didn't make the Top 100, but they're worth playing if you're in the area.

(Listed alphabetically)

DEBARY GOLF & COUNTRY CLUB

300 Plantation Club Dr., DeBary
407-668-2061; Par: 72; Yards: 6,776–5,060.
Access: Open to the public; Green fees: Under $40.

Lloyd Clifton designed this nice course with rolling fairways and tree-lined fairways. The greens are excellent and the course has hosted some PGA qualifying tournaments.

GRENELEFE GOLF & TENNIS RESORT, EAST COURSE

3200 S.R. 546, Haines City
813-422-7511; Par: 72; Yards: 6,802–5,114.
Access: Open to the public; Green fees: $50 to $99.

The shortest of the three courses at the resort, the East course was designed by Arnold Palmer and Ed Seay. It is tight and with many doglegs and twisting fairways.

THE HABITAT GOLF COURSE

3591 Fairgreen St., Valkaria
407-952-4588; Par: 72; Yards: 6,836–4,969.
Access; Open to the public; Green fees: Under $50.

A good course in a wonderful setting. The Habitat is less than five years old and will mature into a very good course.

KISSIMMEE BAY COUNTRY CLUB

2801 Kissimmee Bay Blvd., Kissimmee
407-348-4653; Par: 71; Yards: 6,846–5,171.
Access: Open to the public; Green fees: Under $65.

Set in a natural setting amid massive oak trees, this Lloyd Clifton-designed course features fast greens that are cut twice a day. The 166-yard par No. 16 has a beautiful view of a lake.

LAS COLINAS COURSE, MISSION INN

10400 Country Road 48, Howey-in-the-Hills
904-324-3101; Par: 72; Yards: 6,867–4,500.
Access: Open to the public; Green fees: $50 to $90.

Las Colinas is nothing like its sister Campeon Course. Las Colinas is flat and wide open, giving you much more room to spray your tee and approach shots.

LINKS OF LAKE BERNADETTE

813-788-7888; Par: 71; Yards: 6,392–5,031.
Access: Open to the public; Green fees: Under $40.

Combining a good blend of lakes, bunkers and pampas grass, Lake Bernadette creates a rugged look. This doesn't mean the course is not well-maintained. You will also need to keep the ball in play here, because there is lots of lateral trouble.

MARRIOTT'S ORLANDO WORLD CENTER

World Center Drive, Orlando
407-238-8659; Par: 71; Yards: 6,307-5,048.
Access: Open to the public; Green fees: $50 to $100.

A tight Joe Lee design, this course set around the 27-story hotel. The short length is deceiving because there is water on 16 holes and 85 bunkers to penalize any errant shots.

RIDGEWOOD LAKES

101 Spanish Moss Rd., Davenport
813-424-8688; Par: 72; Yards: 7,016–5,217.
Access: Open to the public; Green fees: Under $50.

This Red McAnlis design has prompted much talk because of all the forced carries over water and wetlands. Many of the greens are bulkheaded and the wet stuff is a factor on 15 holes. There are four sets of tees on every hole, so pick the right one.

SANDPIPER GOLF & COUNTRY CLUB

6001 Sandpiper Dr., Lakeland
813-859-5461; Par: 70; Yards: 6,450–5,024.
Access: Open to the public; Green fees: Under $40.

A course few people outside Lakeland know about, it is very popular among local residents for its great prices and fun layout. A Scottish-style course with little water, Sandpiper has lots of sand. It had too much, so some of the fairway waste areas were grassed to make the course more playable.

SEVEN HILLS GOLFERS CLUB

10599 Fairchild Dr., Spring Hill
904-688-8888; Par: 72; Yards: 6,715–4,902.
Access: Open to the public; Green fees: Under $60.

About an hour north of Tampa, this is a nice, scenic course that not many people know about. There is rolling fairways and nice, fast greens.

SEVILLE GOLF & COUNTRY CLUB

18200 Seville Clubhouse Dr., Brooksville
813-596-7888; Par: 72; Yards: 7,140–5,236.
Access: Open to the public; Green fees: Under $60.

Tucked away in a secluded spot northwest of Tampa, Seville features gently rolling hills and fairways lined with oaks and pine trees. There are large bunkers with gaping faces.

COUNTRY CLUB OF SILVER SPRINGS SHORES

565 Silver Rd., Ocala
904-687-2828; Par: 72; Yards: 6,857–5,188.
Access: Open to the public; Green fees: Under $50.

Set amid a forest of oak trees and pristine lakes, this course has nice rolling fairways and plenty of bunkers.

SPRING LAKE GOLF & TENNIS RESORT

100 Clubhouse Lane, Sebring
813-655-0101; Par: 36/36/36; Yards: 3,128–3,400–3,270.
Access: Open to the public; Green fees: Under $50.

Three well-maintained nines that are fairly wide open. No. 9 on the Osprey 9 claims to be the world's largest green. It covers more than an acre.

WALT DISNEY WORLD, LAKE BUENA VISTA COURSE

2200 Club Lake Dr., Lake Buena Vista
407-824-2270; Par: 72; Yards: 6,829–5,176.
Access: Open to the public; Green fees: $50 to $100.

Of the original three Disney courses (Magnolia and Palm are the others) this is the tightest of the Joe Lee designs. It was closed in 1993–94 for renovations and is much better now.

NORTHEAST REGION

Sure, the state's top-ranked course is here. But there is much more. This is the golf resort capital of the state. The five top courses in the region are all resort courses. If you are course-hopping, there is plenty for you to play.

From the new LPGA course in Daytona Beach to the steep elevation changes at Ravines just south of Jacksonville, the region has some of the most varied terrain for golf courses in Florida.

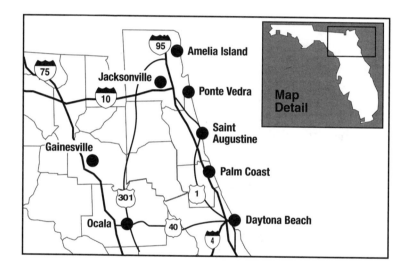

COURSES IN THE TOP 100

These courses made the list of the Top 100 courses in the state. You'll find more information about them under their respective listings in the top 100 section of this book.

1   TPC–STADIUM COURSE

1000 TPC Boulevard, Ponte Vedra Beach
(904) 285-7777; Par: 72; Yards: 6,857–5,034.
Access: Marriott resort guests only; Green fees: $100 and up.

Pete Dye masterpiece has it all. Home of the PGA Tour's Players Championship.

5   LONG POINT, AMELIA ISLAND PLANTATION

Highway A1A South, Amelia Island
(904) 277-5907; Par: 72; Yards: 6,775-4,927.
Access: Amelia Island Plantation resort guests only.
Green fees: $80 to $100.

The best natural setting for a golf course in Florida. Designed by Tom Fazio.

13   SAWGRASS COUNTRY CLUB, MARRIOTT AT SAWGRASS RESORT

10034 Golf Club Dr., Ponte Vedra Beach
(904) 273-3720; Par: 72; Yards: 6,900-5,128.
Access: Resort guests only; Green fees: $100 and up.

A very challenging layout that used to be the home of the PGA Tour's Players Championship.

16   AMELIA LINKS, AMELIA ISLAND PLANTATION

Highway A1A South, Amelia Island
(800) 874-6878; Par: 36/36/36.
Yards: Oakmarsh—3,308–2,560; Oysterbay—3,194–2,498; Oceanside—2,832–2,231.
Access: Resort guests only; Green fees: $65–$85.

Three distinct nines worth playing. Oceanside has three consecutive holes along the ocean.

19 GOLF CLUB OF AMELIA ISLAND

4700 Amelia Island Parkway, Amelia Island
(904) 277-8015; Par: 72; Yards: 6,681–5,039.
Access: Guests of the Ritz-Carlton and Summer Beach Resort.
Green fees: $50 to $100.

A wonderful setting for a golf course.

21 LPGA INTERNATIONAL

300 Champions Dr., Daytona Beach
(904) 274-3880; Par: 72; Yards: 7,088–5,744.
Access: Open to the public; Green fees: $25 to $60.

Rees Jones created a nice course from flat land. Site of LPGA
Sprint Championships.

31 RAVINES GOLF CLUB

2932 Ravines Road, Middleburg
(904) 282-7888; Par: 72; Yards: 6,733–4,817.
Access: Open to the public; Green fees: Under $50.

A wonderful mountain course in Florida. Probably the most fun
you will have playing golf in Florida.

41 WINDSOR PARKE

4747 Hodges Blvd., Jacksonville
(904) 223-GOLF; Par: 72; Yards: 6,740–5,206
Access: Open to the public; Green fees: Under $75.

A well-maintained course surrounded by tall pines.

43 QUEEN'S HARBOUR

13361 Atlantic Blvd., Jacksonville
904-221-1012; Par: 72; Yards: 7,012–5,139.
Access: Open to the public; Green fees: $30 to $60.

A fun course to play along the Intracoastal Waterway.

No. 4 on the TPC–Valley Course, which is next to the Stadium Course.

44 CIMARRONE

2690 Cimarrone Blvd., Jacksonville
(904) 287-2000; Par: 72; Yards: 6,891–4,707.
Access: Open to the public; Green fees: Under $60.

Excellent setting with water on 17 holes.

47 TPC–VALLEY COURSE

1000 TPC Blvd., Ponte Vedra Beach
(904) 285-7777; Par: 72; Yards: 6,864–5,126.
Access: Resort guests only; Green fees: $100 and up.

Next door to the Stadium Course, site of the Senior PGA Players Championship.

54 MATANZAS WOODS

398 Lakeview Blvd., Palm Coast
904-446-6330; Par: 72; Yards: 6,985–5,348.
Access: Open to the public; Green fees: $39 to $52.

The best of the four courses at Sheraton Palm Coast, it was designed by Arnold Palmer.

65 INDIGO LAKES

2620 W. International Speedway, Daytona Beach
904-254-3607; Par: 72; Yards: 7,168–5,159.
Access: Open to the public. Green fees: Under $50.

Former site of an LPGA Tour event.

67 HALIFAX PLANTATION

4000 Old Dixie Hwy., Ormond Beach
904-676-9600; Par: 72; Yards: 7,128–4,971.
Access: Open to the public; Green fees: Under $40.

A fun course in a very nice wooded setting.

80 GOLF CLUB OF JACKSONVILLE

10440 Tournament Lane, Jacksonville
904-779-0800; Par: 71; Yards: 6,620–5,021.
Access: Open to the public; Green fees: Under $50.

One of the few public courses still managed by the PGA Tour.

82 OCEAN COURSE, PONTE VEDRA INN AND CLUB

200 Ponte Vedra Blvd., Ponte Vedra Beach
904-285-1111; Par: 72; Yards: 6,515–5,230.
Access: Open to the public; Green fees: $50 to $100.

An excellent old Robert Trent Jones course with what is believed to be the first island green.

85 PONCE DE LEON GOLF & CONFERENCE RESORT

4000 U.S. Highway 1 North, St. Augustine
904-829-5314; Par: 72; Yards: 6,878–5,315.
Access: Open to the public; Green fees: $50 to $100.

One of the first courses to open in Florida (in 1916), it is a Donald Ross classic.

OTHER NOTABLE COURSES IN THE NORTHEAST FLORIDA REGION

These courses didn't make the Top 100, but they're worth playing if you're in the area.

(Listed alphabetically)

CHAMPIONS CLUB AT JULINGTON CREEK

1111 Durbin Creek Blvd., Jacksonville
904-287-GOLF; Par: 72; Yards: 6,872–4,994.
Access; Open to the public; Green fees: Under $75.

A well-maintained course designed by Steve Melnyk that meanders through the woods. There are also wetlands and 40 bunkers to negotiate.

GOLF CLUB AT CYPRESS HEAD

6231 Whispering Lake, Port Orange
904-756-5449; Par: 72; Yards: 6,814–4,971.
Access: Open to the public; Green fees: Under $40.

A new course designed by Arthur Hills, Cypress Head brings water and/or wetlands into play on almost every hole. The greens are very good and the green fees are among the best bargains in the region.

CYPRESS KNOLL

53 E. Hampton Blvd., Palm Coast
904-437-5807; Par: 72; Yards: 6,591–5,386.
Access: Open to the public; Green fees: Under $50.

Located between Jacksonville and Daytona Beach, this is a hard, tight course that demands precision.

DEERCREEK COUNTRY CLUB

7816 McLaurin Rd., Jacksonville
904-363-1507; Par: 72; Yards: 7,003–5282.
Access: Open to the public; Green fees: Under $60.

Deercreek has a secluded location surrounded by trees that frame almost every green. There is also plenty of water. The course is also bordered by a 285-acre natural preserve.

EAGLE HARBOR GOLF CLUB

2217 Eagle Harbor Parkway, Orange Park
904-269-9300; Par: 72; Yards: 6,840–4,980.
Access: Open to the public; Green fees: Under $40.

The course is cut through 60-foot tall pine trees, creating a serene setting. There is plenty of water to keep your attention on the game and a unique island putting game to help you practice.

MILL COVE GOLF CLUB

1700 Monument Rd., Jacksonville
904-646-4653; Par: 71; Yards: 6,622–4,719.
Access: Open to the public; Green fees: Under $50.

Located in northeast Jacksonville, this course has rolling fairways, wetlands and marsh areas. Many of the fairways are lined with tall pines.

RIVER BEND GOLF CLUB

730 Airport Road, Ormond Beach
904-673-6000; Par: 72; Yards: 6,821–5,112.
Access: Open to the public; Green fees: Under $50.

This is a pretty golf course with great rates and fairways in excellent shape. It is located near Daytona Beach.

ST. JOHN'S COUNTY GOLF COURSE

4900 Cypress Links Blvd., Elkton
904-825-4900; Par: 72; Yards: 6,926–5,137.
Access: Open to the public; Green fees: Under $20.

This is a fine course with few trees and lots of room. There are plenty of birds hanging around and some water to keep your attention on the game. Some of the greens are bulkheaded.

SUGAR MILL COUNTRY CLUB

100 Clubhouse Circle, New Smyrna Beach
904-426-5210; Par: 36/36/36; Yards: 3,536–3,410–3,339.
Access: Open to the public; Green fees: Under $40.

Joe Lee designed these long and narrow nines located just south of Daytona Beach. Tall trees provide the backdrop on many greens and several lakes provide challenges throughout the round.

NORTHWEST REGION

If you're looking for a place to hit the beach and the links on the same day, this is the region. From the 63 holes at Sandestin to the myriad of courses less than 15 minutes from the Gulf of Mexico, there are plenty of options.

The best concentration of courses lies between Pensacola and Panama City Beach, although there are some excellent courses in both of those cities.

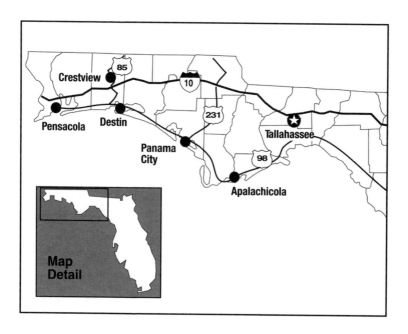

COURSES IN THE TOP 100

These courses made the list of the Top 100 courses in the state. You'll find more information about them under their respective listings in the top 100 section of this book.

9   BURNT PINE GOLF CLUB, SANDESTIN RESORT
5500 Highway 98 East, Destin
(904) 267-6500; Par: 72; Yards: 7,046–5,096.
Access: Limited access to Sandestin Resort guests.
Green fees: Under $75.

Rees Jones' latest creation is the best in Northeast Florida.

12   LAGOON LEGEND, MARRIOTT BAY POINT RESORT
100 Delwood Beach Road, Panama City Beach
(904) 235-6937; Par: 72; Yards: 6,885–4,942.
Access: Open to the public, discount for resort guests.
Green fees: Under $75.

Probably the toughest course in Florida. There is water everywhere.

26   BAYTOWNE, SANDESTIN RESORT
9300 Highway 98 West
(904) 267-8155;
Par: 36/36/36; Yards: Harbor/Troon—6,891–4,884;
Troon/Dunes –7,185-5,158; Dunes/Harbor—6,890–4,862.
Access: Open to the public; Green fees: $55 to $75.

Three very good nines at one of the state's best oceanfront resorts.

32   EMERALD BAY
40001 Emerald Coast Parkway, Destin
(904) 837-5197; Par: 72; Yards: 6,802–5,184.
Access: Open to the public; Green fees: $50 to $90.

Located in a nice, secluded setting next to the bay.

Water is very common on the Links course at Sandestin Resort.

42 HIDDEN CREEK

307 PGA Blvd., Navarre
(904) 939-4604; Par: 72; Yards: 6,862–5,213.
Access: Open to the public; Green fees: Under $50.

Ron Garl produced a solid test of golf. Not much water, nice trees.

46 THE GOLF CLUB AT BLUEWATER BAY

1950 Bluewater Blvd., Niceville
(904) 897-3241; Par: 36/36/36/36.
Yardage: Bay—3,318–2,630; Lake–3,485–2,748;
Marsh—3,362–2,544;
Magnolia—3,307–2,499.
Access: Open to the public; Green fees: Under $50.

The course has grown from 18 to 36 holes, with 27 of them designed by Tom Fazio.

49 MOORS

3220 Avalon Blvd., Milton
(904) 995-GOLF; Par: 71; Yards: 6,912–5,340.
Access: Open to the public; Green fees: Under $65.

Scottish-style course that is site of Senior PGA Tour event.

51 MARCUS POINTE

2500 Oak Pointe Drive, Pensacola
904-484-9770; Par: 72; Yards: 6,737–5,252.
Access: Open to the public; Green fees: Under $40.

The fairways are lined with tall pines and old oaks.

58 LINKS COURSE, SANDESTIN

5500 Emerald Coast Parkway East, Destin
904-267-8144. Par: 72. Yards: 6,710–4,969.
Access: Open to the public; discount to resort guests.
Green fees: $55 to $75.

The course has very nice bay views from several holes and is fun to play.

74 EAST COURSE, TIGER POINT GOLF AND COUNTRY CLUB

1255 Country Club Rd., Gulf Breeze
904-932-1333. Par: 72. Yards: 7,033–5,209.
Access: Open to the public. Green fees: Under $50.

This is unusual: a par 4 with a bunker in the middle of the green.

96 HOMBRE GOLF CLUB

120 Coyote Pass, Panama City Beach
904-234-3673. Par: 72. Yards: 6,820–4,800.
Access: Open to the public. Green fees: $40 to $75.

This course will put a lot of pressure on your game off the tee.

100 CLUB MEADOWS, MARRIOTT BAY POINT RESORT

100 Delwood Beach Road, Panama City Beach
904-235-6909; Par: 72; Yards: 6,913–4,999.
Access: Open to the public; Green fees: $50 to $100.

Sister course to Lagoon Legend (No. 12), this one is more wide open and much easier.

OTHER NOTABLE COURSES IN THE NORTHWEST FLORIDA REGION

These courses didn't make the Top 100, but they're worth playing if you're in the area.

(Listed alphabetically)

INDIAN BAYOU GOLF AND COUNTRY CLUB (SEMINOLE/CHOCTAW/CREEK NINES)

1 Country Club Road, Destin
904-837-6191. Par: 36/36/36. Yards: 3,541/3,417/3,475.
Access: Open to the public. Green fees: Under $50.

Three good nines, all with lots of sands. Creek is the newest nine.

KILLEARN COUNTRY CLUB & INN, SOUTH/NORTH/EAST NINES

100 Tyron Circle, Tallahassee
904- 893-2144. Par: 36/36/36. Yards: 3,532/3,493/3,367.
Access: Hotel guests only.

The site of an LPGA Tour event until 1993, Killearn is the antithesis of the mega golf resort. With only 49 rooms and a small conference center, the resort has country charm and 27 holes of good golf. The setting is private and serene, the golf understated and unpretentious.

Set along rolling fairways along oak-lined fairways, Killearn has a Georgia feel. Forced carries are minimal and there is not an abundance of water.

MAGNOLIA OAKS

5248 Clubhouse Dr., Marianna
904-482-8787. Par: 72; Yards: 6,951–5,152.
Access: Open to the public. Green Fees: Under $25.

The course recently changed management and is upgrading the conditions on this oak-lined layout.

OAKS COURSE, FORT WALTON BEACH MUNICIPAL

1909 Lewis Turner Blvd., Fort Walton Beach
904-862-0933. Par: 72. Yards: 6,416–4,992.
Access: Open to the public. Green fees: Under $30.

One of the better municipal courses in the state. You can walk anytime and there is not much trouble. No. 3 is a dogleg left par 5 with water in front of the green. There is a creek that snakes through the property, cutting across the fairways of Nos. 2, 7, 12 and twice on No. 15—in front of the tee and then in front of the green.

The course is heavily wooded and is home to the original Edwin Watts golf store, which is still open next to the starter's hut.

PERDIDO BAY RESORT

1 Doug Ford Dr., Pensacola
904-492-1223. Par: 72. Yards: 7,154–5,476.
Access: Open to the public. Green fees: Under $50.

The home of the Pensacola Open from 1978 to 1987. Curtis Strange won his first PGA Tour event here in 1979. The course ran into financial problems some years ago, but is now rebounding. The course is fairly flat and wide open, but there is water on 16 of the 18 holes.

PINES COURSE, FORT WALTON BEACH MUNICIPAL

1909 Lewis Turner Blvd., Fort Walton Beach
904-862-3314. Par: 72. Yards: 6,802–5,320.
Access: Open to the public. Green fees: Under $30.

Located just north of the Oaks Course and with its own starter's hut, the Pines Course is a little more wide open, less wooded and with less water. Water only comes into play on Nos. 6, 7, 14 and 15. There are some nice touches not usually found on a "muny," such as bulkheaded water hazards.

The prettiest hole is the par 5 sixth, which snakes left slightly and a little downhill to a bulkheaded green guarded by water in front. The green is large and the big mound behind the green frames it nicely.

SANTA ROSA GOLF & BEACH CLUB

4838 West County Highway 30-A, Santa Rosa
904-267-2229. Par: 72. Yards: 6,608–4,920.
Access: Open to the public. Green fees: Under $35.

A no-nonsense layout with nine holes overlooking the Gulf of Mexico. The course is four miles east of the Sandestin resort and very close to the beach.

SEASCAPE RESORT

100 Seascape Dr., Destin
904-654-7888. Par: 71. Yards: 6,488–5,047.
Access: Open to the public; discount for resort guests.
Green fees: Under $50.

A small, charming resort on the beach, Seascape is run by the same folks who run the more demanding Emerald Bay (No. 34 on Florida's Top 100 Courses). The course is short, but water forces you to hit the ball straight to score well. Nos. 6, 14 and 17 are all sharp doglegs around lakes.

SHALIMAR POINTE GOLF & COUNTRY CLUB

302 Country Club Rd., Shalimar
904-651-1416. Par: 72. Yards: 6,765–5,427.
Access: Open to the public. Green fees: Under $50.

Joe Finger designed this course along the Choctawhatchee Bay, north of Ft. Walton Beach. In 1985, Pete Dye came in and added some refinements—more waste bunkers and bulkheaded the water hazards. The course now looks better and plays tougher.

The short par 4 (335 yards) No. 14 is the best hole. A dogleg right, the fairway has a huge waste bunker protecting the bend. The peninsula green is undulating and guarded by water.

SHOAL RIVER COUNTRY CLUB

1100 Shoal River Dr., Crestview
904-689-1111. Par: 72. Yards: 6,782–5,183.
Access: Open to the public. Green fees: Under $35.

Come for the greens, which are usually in great shape.

SIGNAL HILL

9615 North Thomas Dr., Panama City Beach
904-234-3218. Par: 71. Yards: 5,617–4,790.
Access: Open to the public. Green Fees: Under $30.

Play the back nine, which winds through some beautiful sand dunes. Course is a two-iron from the beaches.

SUNNY HILLS

1150 Country Club Blvd., Sunny Hills
904-773-3619. Par: 72. Yards: 7,095—4,897.
Access: Open to the public. Green fees: Under $25.

Gene Sarazen was the consultant for the back nine and Ken Venturi designed the front of this course with lots of bunkers and large greens.

INDEX